BEYOND SHAME AND PAIN

FORGIVING YOURSELF AND OTHERS

John Michael Berecz

CSS Publishing Company, Inc., Lima, Ohio

BEYOND SHAME AND PAIN

Copyright © 1998 by
CSS Publishing Company, Inc.
Lima, Ohio

The "clients," illustrating various points in this book, are true-to-life, composite images, created from thirty years of the author's clinical experiences, not actual persons.

Scripture quotations are from the *Holy Bible, New International Version.* Copyright © 1973, 1978, 1984 International Bible Society. Used by permission of Zondervan Bible Publishers. All rights reserved.

Story excerpted from Mark Twain, *The Adventures of Tom Sawyer, Mark Twain Library.* Edited/translated by Paul Baender. Copyright © 1982 The Mark Twain Foundation. Used by permission.

"If a Boder Meets a Boder, Need a Boder Cry? Yes" from *There's Always Another Wind-mill* by Ogden Nash. Copyright © 1967 by Ogden Nash; first appeared in *The New Yorker.* By permission of Little, Brown and Company.

Library of Congress Cataloging-in-Publication Data

Berecz, John M. (John Michael)
  Beyond shame and pain : forgiving yourself and others / John Berecz.
      p.   cm.
    ISBN 0-7880-1183-9 (pbk.)
    1. Forgiveness. 2. Forgiveness—Religious aspects.   I. Title.
BF637.F67B47   1998
179'.9—dc21   97-29449
                                                                                          CIP

ISBN 0-7880-1183-9   PRINTED IN U.S.A.

For Deborah
friend, wife, and foremost forgiver;

for my sons
Michael, Ryan, Lamont, and Jamison
who have given me much to remember, little to forgive;

and for my clients
who have shared with me their pain, joy, and forgiveness.

Also by John M. Berecz, Ph.D.:
Sexual Styles: A Psychologist's Guide
To Understanding Your Lover 's Personality.

Table Of Contents

Introduction

Forgiveness As Taught
By A Dead Dog

It was twilight one late November afternoon. I was driving into town to take care of some business when the question came. It was one of those unanticipated ways in which children provide you with moments that last a lifetime.

We passed a cemetery. The falling snow magically transformed rough granite monuments and neglected headstones into delicate art forms. I hardly noticed as I carefully titrated the distance between my car and the taillights in front of me on the rapidly slickening roadway.

"Dad?" a voice from the rear seat.

"Yeah?"

"When Satan dies will God put flowers on his grave?"

"Uh ... yeah, I think so ... uh, yes, He will, I'm sure He will," I stammered.

Not the kind of question you find answered in the "how-to-parent" books. Not the kind of issue most of us spend much time thinking about. Michael had never been loquacious, preferring observation to verbalization, but when he did ask questions they were frequently thought-provoking. But this time I got more than I bargained for when I asked him if he wanted to ride to town with me. "What possesses kids to ask such questions?" I wondered.

Then it hit me. A few weeks earlier tragedy had struck the heart of our family. Nina, our Great Dane, had died. Abruptly. Without warning. I was returning home from work when she ran to the edge of the driveway happily barking to greet me. Suddenly — midbark — she collapsed. As I jumped out of the car and rushed to her side, the boys, playing in the yard, were horrified. They watched, pale-faced, silently, as I looked for signs of life, but there was no movement of her giant rib cage. Desperately, I put my ear to her chest. Silence.

"She's dead, boys."

I announced it with all the contrived casualness I could muster. "No use calling the vet; nothing he can do."

But such a cruel reality required some cushioning — something to soften the harsh edges for young boys ages five, seven, and nine. It required some softening for a dad age 37.

"I'll run into town and get some flowers, then we'll bury her in the backyard. You guys pick some wildflowers. I'll be back in twenty minutes."

We had a graveside ceremony. I no longer remember exactly what I said, but the memory of three small boys bravely huddling around a Great-Dane-sized heap of fresh earth, each clutching wildflowers in one fist and a long-stemmed rose in the other, still has a painful edge twenty years later.

As Michael and I drove along the snowy highway a few weeks later, the snow-enhanced headstones and crosses must have reminded him of his dead doggy and of the flowers we'd put on her grave. He couched his question in familiar Judeo-Christian terms. Taught to believe that God is good and will ultimately overcome evil (Satan), Michael didn't question that axiom of his belief system; rather he raised the more important question *how?* Will it be with compassion? Is God forgiving? Will he put flowers on Satan's (Hitler's — name your villain) grave?

Not a bad question to ponder. In fact, it is the central question of this book. How does God deal with bad events and bad people? How can you? If you're not "religious" please don't stop reading now, because this book isn't primarily for devout believers who worry about fixing the wrongs they've committed. For them, forgiveness means that God has audited their moral accounts and with the help of "amazing grace" has balanced their books. But it's not only "sinners" who need compassion. Forgiveness is too important to reserve only for the religious.

We all try to make sense of the good and bad in our lives, and no matter whether we think theologically, philosophically, or psychologically, clear answers are difficult to obtain. In quiet moments questions hover like mist over placid ponds in the cool morning air. "Will God plant flowers on Satan's grave?" "Is Hitler in heaven

8

or hell?" "Was Schindler a sociopath or a savior?" "Am I in balance — Yin and Yang in equilibrium?" "Is my inner child drowning in toxic shame?" "Do I know my angel?" When the sun shines brightly, or breezes blow gently, our fog seems temporarily to recede, but with darkness and quiet, the questions always return.

Scholars of all stripes have grappled with the great eternal opposites — good and evil — for centuries, so I won't pretend to solve such complex problems with easy-to-follow advice. However, as a practicing clinical psychologist, I would like to share with you what I've learned over the past thirty years about coping with bad things. I've come to believe that forgiveness is at the heart of healing. Before we go further let me define what I mean by forgiving.

To forgive is to let go of past mistakes — your mistakes, the mistakes of others.

It means dumping your excess baggage — trunks filled with shame and guilt about your own badness, suitcases of bitterness and rage toward others. No, you can't, as the trite phrase has it, *"forgive and forget"* — but you can travel more lightly. Briefcase and carry on.

"Sounds good!" you say, as you cautiously consider my travel plans. "But how? ... How do I 'just let go'?" Good question. That's where I would like to help. I would like to share some ideas of *how* you can let go of the past, *how* you can travel more lightly. The remainder of the book is devoted to that, but you are entitled to a preview, so here goes.

I begin not with how to forgive others, but how to forgive *yourself*. This is by far the more difficult journey. It's not coincidental that I refer to "trunks" of shame about yourself and "suitcases" of bitterness toward others.

Like many of your friends and most of my clients, you probably have enormous problems forgiving yourself. This gets unconsciously projected onto others or externalized in surreptitious ways so that you even fool yourself into thinking that all is "forgiven and forgotten." So I begin with a discussion of how to forgive yourself. This will help you to like (and forgive) yourself better.

Next I examine the topic of free will, personal responsibility, and blaming. Although this sounds philosophically abstruse and irrelevant to "life in the trenches," it forms an important foundation for genuinely forgiving others. If I believe your behavior is freely chosen — that you've used your "willpower" to make a decision — I'm much more likely to hold you *responsible* (code for "blame you") for your behavior. The five-year-old's protests — "He started it!" "It's her fault!" "I was just hitting back!" — echo through the years. But if I begin to understand your past history — how your parents treated you, how playmates responded to your attempts to be friendly, how people responded when you apologized, and so forth — I will usually be less judgmental and less willing to attribute "free choice" to your every action — less willing to "blame" you. I'll be more forgiving.

In daily life forgiving is not a static formulistic ritual. It is, rather, a dynamic expression of how you relate to yourself and others. Your *forgiving style* is a special case of your *personality style*; in short, it is a window on your inner life. Consequently, I will discuss several personality styles, illustrating how personality colors forgiving.

Finally we will discuss some illustrative examples of religious/spiritual forgiveness, with particular emphasis on styles and personalities of both the forgiving and forgiven.

This background will, I trust, make it easier for you to *let go* of those things which impede your psychological growth and interfere with social relationships. I think it will be an exciting journey. I hope you'll "book" it.

Figure 1

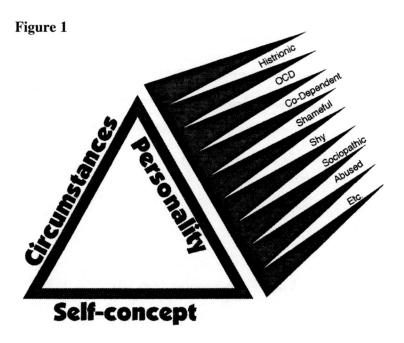

In this book I have chosen to focus on three components of forgiveness which dynamically interact to shape how we dispense mercy to ourselves and others. Each component can be represented as one of the sides of a triangle, each radiating toward the center where the components all meld into a person's unique blend of forgiveness.

In this model, pictured in Figure 1, **self-concept**, **circumstances**, and **personality style** all interact to shape each person's unique mix of forgiveness.

Chapter one explores how **self-concept** influences our forgiving. For example, a man who was constantly criticized as a child would likely have a diminished view of himself and would find it very difficult to forgive someone who disparaged him or reprimanded him in any way.

Chapter two examines the complexities of **circumstances** and how we often oversimply situations when we blame others. In the circumstance of a plane crash, it is seldom easy to ascertain which of the numerous circumstances — pilot error, engine failure, blinding snow, iced wings, and so forth — may have caused the crash. Similarly, when human behavior "crashes" it is usually due to a complex of circumstances, not easily disentangled. Consequently, we ought to be slower to judge and blame, and more inclined to forgive.

Chapters three, four, five, six, and seven consider how **personality styles** shape forgiveness. For example, a woman with a co-dependent personality might marry a man with an evil temper with the hope of transforming him. Then she might endure his repeated assaults upon her, "forgiving" him each time, saying she loved him too much to separate. But though she might appear to be giving him the gold of forgiveness, it is rather the "fool's gold" of co-dependency, glittering like love, but driven by a personality filled with insecurity.

Chapter eight offers two illustrative case studies. The first, about a woman who was severely sexually abused as a child and teen, illustrates how, even in such a horrible circumstance, one can forgive others. The other, about a woman who was nearly destroyed by the guilt of her abortion, illustrates how one can forgive self.

Chapter nine explains the pivotal concept of psychological **reframing**, using common illustrations from the lives of such dissimilar persons as Tom Sawyer and Jesus Christ.

Chapter 1

How *Self-Esteem* Shapes Forgiveness

Known as the "Narcotics Farm" or NARCO, the hospital is situated on 900 acres of rolling countryside near Lexington, Kentucky. It serves as a treatment center for opiate addicts and polydrug abusers.

"Bill, a short man, was asked to move by Wendell, an extremely tall, muscular individual. Bill, sensitive about his size, thought he detected an insult in Wendell's voice. While Bill knew he was in the way, he refused to move and challenged Wendell to move him. The two were stopped just short of a fight. At a minimum, each risked leaving the hospital and returning to prison; at a maximum, death, for each acknowledged that he had been prepared to kill the other. Bill later explained in group, 'I'm nothing, but it would kill me to let those suckers know it. I've got to show them all the time. It would just kill me if they knew. Then I'd really be nothing.' " (Wishnie, 1977, p. 41)

Self-esteem in such people is so fragile that it must be constantly protected — at all times and at all costs. Life-and-death struggles develop at NARCO over a game of pool, a place in line, or a book of matches. When counseled individually such people refer to themselves as failures.

There is no single type of drug abuser. Most suffer from a variety of problems, yet each shares in common a sense of personal hopelessness which the addict tries to avoid through the use of narcotics or stimulants. One patient who had been on a six-month binge of alcohol and drugs and ended up hooked on heroin explained, "What's the use? It's hopeless. It's like I'm empty inside. There is nothing that will make it better." (Wishnie, 1977, p. 173)

People with emotional problems come in an infinite variety of personality types. Like fingerprints, no two are alike. But I've learned through clinical experience that poor self-esteem permeates most forms of emotional pathology — people don't like themselves. This is true of drug-addicted patients, it's true of the severely schizophrenic, and it's true of nearly everyone in between.

Silvano Arieti, one of the world's leading authorities on schizophrenia, describes the delusional and hallucinatory experiences of patients as follows:

> *A patient has the idea that people laugh at him. He actually hears them laughing, and he turns his head; he looks at them and sees them smiling and ridiculing him. They may not smile at all, and he may misinterpret their facial expressions. If they do smile, they may do so for reasons that have nothing to do with him. Again we must help the patient to recognize that he sees or hears people laughing at him when he expects to see them ... However, when the treatment is more advanced, the patient recognizes that he feels people **should** laugh at him because he is a laughable individual. He hears them laughing because he believes that they should laugh at him. What he thinks of himself becomes the cause of his symptoms ... Unless the patient changes his vision of himself, he is not likely to lose his psychosis or the potentiality for psychosis. (Arieti, 1974, pp. 576, 593)*

Unfortunately, disliking oneself is not confined to people with drug addictions, hallucinations, or other clinical problems. The epidemic of self-dislike has not skipped over Christians or Jews, Catholics or Protestants. It is something we all struggle with. Few people can pass the "mirror test." Can you?

Right now, look at yourself in the mirror of your mind. Do you like what you see? Can you honestly say to your inner self, "You're a fine person — I like you!" If you can, you need read no further. You might return this book to your bookseller for a refund or give it to a friend. Most of us, however, long to feel better about ourselves.

Love Begins At Home

It is difficult to love others, including God, if you dislike yourself. And it is almost impossible to forgive yourself for the mistakes of everyday life if you chronically dislike yourself. If your self-esteem is too low — below a healthy psychological "sea level" — you will tend to siphon attention and social interactions back toward yourself in an attempt to prop up your sagging self-image. You won't have much love to give others because you'll be so concerned about getting enough for yourself. If, on the other hand, you like yourself and feel adequate, you'll have something special (yourself) to share with others. Healthy self-love is based on the security one feels from being loved by significant others early in life. This kind of love flows outward to others. Conspicuously absent is the need to be constantly admired, praised, or celebrated by others.

When Christ succinctly summarized all of scripture into a triangle of love for God, others, and ourselves (Matthew 22:37-39), I don't think he was suggesting any kind of hierarchy — that *first* we ought to love God, *secondly* others, and *lastly* ourselves. Although theologically speaking, God is certainly primary in this triangle, *psychologically* we must *first* love ourselves if we are ever to love others or God. Developmentally the order is exactly reversed from how we usually hear preachers talk about it! Similarly, we must be able to forgive *ourselves* if we are genuinely to forgive others.

Comparing Ourselves With Others

There are numerous reasons for low self-esteem, but one of the most common reasons many of us dislike ourselves is that we attempt to create self-esteem out of performance. We live in a culture which emphasizes achievement as the basis for acceptance. It is the bane of our existence that we think we are good people only when we do a good job, get good grades, or perform admirably in athletic events.

This is intensified by a tendency to compare ourselves with one another. This is hardly a new phenomenon; the Olympics began centuries ago with the Greeks. But what is particularly destructive about contemporary culture is that in the process of being entertained, or informed, the media persistently prod me to compare myself with others who are more beautiful, more successful, more powerful, more intelligent, and more charming. I always come out a poor second. Try as I might I can't play golf like Jack Nicklaus or Tiger Woods. I can't interview as well as Barbara Walters, nor is my counsel as witty as that dispensed by Ann Landers. Too often, in today's adolescent jargon, I'm a "loser."

Even the joyous yuletide season has been clouded with a comparison device known as the "Christmas Letter." Again, I find I'm running near the back of the pack, because while my kids are struggling through remedial reading, Aunt Heather lets me know that Brandon is graduating with honors. My college roommate, now a successful physician, can't resist reporting how he has been able to avoid the hassles of the local racquet club by installing a lighted tennis court in his back yard — just behind the pool!

The apostle Paul recognized the futility of comparing ourselves with others when he counseled: "Each one should test his own actions. Then he can take pride in himself, without comparing himself to somebody else ..." (Galatians 6:4).

Tripod Of Self-Esteem

As we've seen, numerous factors in contemporary culture conspire to sabotage our self-esteem. In order to cope with these influences it is important to understand how self-esteem is shaped. Imagine a camera with which you "picture" your self-esteem, sitting on a tripod. Each of the three legs of the tripod is necessary to provide a stable, steady base for your self-portrait. The legs are basic human condition, self-concept, and self-worth. Each is distinct, yet they all contribute to the total picture we have of ourselves. Let's look at each separately:

Basic Human Condition. As we've noted, our dislike of self is promoted by our contemporary culture. Additionally, however, many sincere people believe that the **basic human condition** is quite bad. It is widely believed by many religious people that we are born into a broken ("sinful") world and that our natural propensity is toward destructiveness ("evil"). We are accurately described, they maintain, by the angel to the church of Laodicea as "wretched, pitiful, poor, blind and naked" (Revelation 3:17). Humanistic writers intensely disagree, contending that with appropriate acceptance and adequate nurturance a wonderful creature will "bloom."

I think both views are a bit extreme. There **are** good tendencies that flourish in the soil of family love, but only when balanced with boundaries and tempered with discipline.

Our basic condition is not as good as the humanists would like to believe, nor as dire as hellfire-and-brimstone preachers or evening news commentators would lead us to believe. Admittedly, neither history nor current events seem to support the optimism of humanists regarding our basic condition. The history of the Holocaust and current conflicts in the Middle East, Northern Ireland, and the former Yugoslavia all seem to suggest that humans are capable of much evil. We need look no further than the inner cities of our sprawling metropolitan regions to find support for the notion that human beings do not always "bloom."

On the other hand, one can still find much that is good, kind, and even heroic in ordinary people in spite of terrible influences. So we might conclude that our basic human condition is not hopelessly permeated with evil, but neither is it blooming with goodness.

Self-concept. How we feel about ourselves is a subjective potpourri which includes past memories, present experiences, and all that goes into what I call "me." I can feel good about "me" or I can feel bad about myself. Most of us intuitively know that this core of self-perceptions colors everything else about life.

Enhancing self-esteem has become something of a cottage industry — spawning workshops, books, and support groups — even influencing educational curricula. I hardly need document the pervasiveness of this in our contemporary society. There's probably little I could add to the burgeoning literature that already exists in this area, so for our current discussion, I'll emphasize that self-esteem is how you *feel* about yourself. It's *not* your basic human condition or your real worth; it's how you *feel*. How you feel about yourself is important, but it comprises only a part of your total self

17

picture. We turn now to real worth, the last of the three legs in our tripod.

Real Worth. This is the area where Judeo-Christian thinking radically departs from other systems of philosophy, psychology, cultural expectations, and even logic. We've seen how contemporary culture establishes personal **worth** in terms of performance. Nowadays if you are young, beautiful or possess intellectual or athletic prowess, in short, if you can "get the job done," you are worth a lot — maybe even an athletic contract that brings in "ten million dollars over four years."

But such self-esteem always feels precarious, as if it is on loan and must be constantly collateralized with excellent performances or else it will be repossessed.

Contrastingly, the gospel tells us that our worth is *not* based on the human condition or on our personal performance. Our worth isn't "on loan" about to be repossessed. Most of us breathe a sigh of relief to hear such news because our yo-yo records of performance don't give us much sense of stability when it comes to self-esteem.

But if our real worth isn't based on performance, what is it based on? Two things: 1) purchase price and 2) family membership.

Real worth, according to Romans 5:8, is completely separate from performance. It's based on *purchase price*: "While we were still sinners [no admirable performance required — it doesn't say "after we graduated" or "upon completing a stint with the Peace Corps"] Christ died for us" [the ultimate purchase price].

If you were to ask me how much my watch is worth, one of the primary considerations would be the original purchase price. Rolex or Timex? Major differences in purchase prices. Peter talks about purchase price in the following way:

> *For you know that it was not with perishable things such as silver or gold that you were redeemed from the empty way of life handed down to you from your forefathers, but with the precious blood of Christ, a lamb without blemish or defect.* (1 Peter 1:18-19)

Family identity is an important measure of how people value themselves and others. If you're a Kennedy or a Vanderbilt, or a child born to Charles and Diana, you're more highly esteemed than "ordinary" citizens. Again, scripture suggests that we can regard ourselves as more than "ordinary."

> *When the time had fully come, God sent his Son, born of a woman, born under law, to redeem those under the law, that we might receive the full rights of sons ... So you are no longer a slave, but a son; and since you are a son, God has made you also an heir.* (Galatians 4:4-7)

The lilting melody of Bill Gaither's song "I'm so Glad I'm a Part of the Family of God" may lull us into missing the enormity of the truth we sing. This family identity is essential to our salvation. We are princes and princesses. Royalty. Children of the King!

It is of interest to note that when tempting Christ in the wilderness the Devil pulled out his biggest guns. He tried to get our Lord to question His family identity: "*If* you are the Son of God, tell these stones to become bread" (Matthew 4:3). "*If* you are the Son of God, throw yourself down" (Matthew 4:6). (italics mine)

But Satan was not successful in causing an identity crisis in Jesus, because just prior to these temptations Christ had received affirmation of His family membership: "This is my Son, whom I love; with him I am well pleased" (Matthew 3:17).

Christ did not doubt His identity, His Sonship, but this is not always the case with us. We too easily forget that we are adopted sons and daughters — part of the family of God.

The outcome of looking at ourselves in the mirror of Scripture is a much more stable sense of self-esteem, because in Scripture, our real worth is based totally on the *price paid* and *family identity*. This is what the eminent preacher Helmut Thielicke refers to as *"alien dignity."* He illustrates with an anecdote:

> *I once saw an illustration of this thought of "alien dignity" when I was in the first form in school. We had there a boy whom we simply could not stand and as is typical at that age we were cooking up a plan to give him*

a thrashing in order to take him down a bit. About the time when this was to take place, I saw his father, who was probably the most distinguished man in our town, one to whom we all looked up, bringing him to school. I saw how he let him off at the gate of the school, put his hand on his head, patted his cheek, and kept waving to him when they parted. It was strange how suddenly this boy changed in my eyes. True, he was still the same somewhat sloppy fellow, but this boy was loved by this man. This gave him in my eyes something like an "alien dignity," not an immanent quality of character or anything else; but this splendor of another's love lay around him. (1962, p. 121)

Thielicke observes: "God loves us, not because we are so valuable; rather we are valuable because God loves us. This is the miracle by which we live." (1962, p. 117)

Notice that such "dignity" comes from the outside. It is self-worth that derives from a locus completely independent of our personal foibles or special achievements. For believers, "specialness" is always initiated by God. "Alien dignity" is not a New Testament concept confined to Christians. At the core of Jewish identity is that same "specialness" because of being loved by God. As an individual, Abraham was chosen:

> *The Lord had said to Abram, "Leave your country, your people and your father's household and go to the land I will show you.*
> *I will make you into a great nation*
> *and I will bless you;*
> *I will make your name great,*
> *and you will be a blessing.*
> *I will bless those who bless you,*
> *and whoever curses you I will curse;*
> *and all peoples on earth*
> *will be blessed through you."* (Genesis 12:1-3)

As a nation, Israel was chosen:

20

The Lord did not set his affection on you and choose you because you were more numerous than other peoples, for you were the fewest of all peoples. But it was because the Lord loved you and kept the oath he swore to your forefathers that he brought you out with a mighty hand and redeemed you from the land of slavery, from the power of Pharaoh king of Egypt. (Deuteronomy 7:7-8)

Throughout scripture — from the Torah to Revelation — the message is the same. God chooses and embraces us, thereby bestowing on us "alien dignity." Consequently, we can steadily feel safe and worthwhile because our self-esteem derives from — to use Thielicke's words — "the splendor of another's love."

We must expand the humanistic mantra "I'm OK, You're OK" by adding a crucial Judeo-Christian dimension, "I'm OK, You're OK — *because He's OK.*"

To say, "I'm OK," really means that I've been chosen.

The believer lives with a dynamic awareness of how loved she is by the Father, and how lonely she is without Him. Along with the prodigal son, we come to an accurate view of ourselves when we simultaneously see both the husks of the pigsty and the house of the Father. The mirror of self will not be found in *People* magazine, television, movies, friends, or work associates. They, like mirrors found in fun houses at carnivals, provide distorted, at times grotesque, reflections of who we really are.

Self-worth and forgiveness are related in the following way. If I like myself and feel some "alien dignity" about who I am, I will find it easier to forgive myself and others when mistakes happen. My self-esteem won't be so fragile that I have to maintain a pretense of perfection in order to like myself.

And if I see myself as one of God's children — all of whom are endowed with the same alien dignity — the boundaries between friends and enemies become blurred. Then it becomes psychologically feasible to follow Christ's seemingly impossible suggestion:

"You have heard that it was said, 'Love your neighbor and hate your enemy.' But I tell you: Love your enemies and pray for those who persecute you, that you may be sons of your Father in heaven." (Matthew 5:43-45)

This is vividly illustrated in Erich Remarque's book about World War I, *All Quiet on the Western Front*. He describes his experiences in a shell-hole:

> *Swiftly I pull out my little dagger, grasp it fast and bury it in my hand once again under the mud. If anyone jumps in here I will go for him; it hammers in my forehead; at once, stab him clean through the throat, so that he cannot call out ... The rattle of machine-guns becomes an unbroken chain. Just as I am about to turn round a little, something heavy stumbles, and with a crash a body falls over me into the shell-hole, slips down, and lies across me — I do not think at all, I make no decision — I strike madly home, and feel only how the body suddenly convulses, then becomes limp, and collapses. When I recover myself, my hand is sticky and wet. The man gurgles ... I want to stop his mouth, stuff it with earth, stab him again, he must be quiet....* (pp. 217-219)

Remarque describes how it feels to be trapped in a shell-hole with an enemy who is slowly dying of the stab wounds he has inflicted:

> *So I crawl away to the farthest corner and stay there, my eyes glued on him, my hand grasping the knife — ready, if he stirs, to spring at him again. But he won't do so anymore, I can hear that already in his gurgling.* (p. 219)

With the grey light of early morning comes a clearer view of the "enemy," who begins to look more human.

> *The figure opposite me moves. I shrink together and involuntarily look at it ... A man with a small pointed beard lies there, his head is fallen to one side, one arm is half-bent, his head rests helplessly upon it ... I unbutton his tunic in order to bandage him if it is possible ... There are three stabs. My field dressing covers them, the blood runs out under it, I press it tighter; he groans. That is all I can do. Now we must wait, wait ... The gurgling starts again — but how slowly a man dies!* (pp. 221-223)

In spite of Remarque's efforts to help, the soldier dies, but in the process of trying to save his life, Remarque finds his "enemy's" humanity grows more compelling.

> *I prop the dead man up again so that he lies comfortably although he feels nothing anymore ... his hair is black and a bit curly at the sides. The mouth is full and soft beneath his moustache ... No doubt his wife still thinks of him; she does not know what has happened. He looks as if he would often have written to her; — she will still be getting mail from him ... I take his wallet in my hand. It slips out of my hand and falls open. Some pictures and letters drop out ... There are portraits of a woman and a little girl, small amateur photographs taken against an ivy-clad wall.* (pp. 224-228)

Remarque confesses to his dead enemy:

> *Comrade, I did not want to kill you. If you jumped in here again, I would not do it ... I see you are a man like me. I thought of your hand-grenades, of your bayonet, of your rifle; now I see your wife and your face and our fellowship. Forgive me, comrade. We always see it too late.* (p. 226)

To love my enemy — to forgive and be forgiven — requires not colossal willpower, nor grit-your-teeth determination, but a radically different point of view. When I regard my "enemy" as my sibling, when I view my antagonist as a brother, my rival as a sister, then healing naturally flows. True, there are some nasty confrontations *within* the family of God (Northern Ireland's Catholic and Protestant Christians come to mind), but sibling rivalry seldom becomes the virulent toxin of racial cleansing or the Holocaust. It's unthinkable to incinerate a family member.

This is the fundamental difference between a Martin Luther King and a Louis Farrakhan or a Mark Furhman. King really believed in the brotherhood/sisterhood of humankind. By Farrakhan or Furhman standards of angry separatism, King was an "Uncle Tom." Few, even among his followers, understood the genius of

23

his *gentle* yet persistent confrontations which served to vilify his white enemies. Night after night television screens carried vivid pictures of white segregationists spitting, sneering, and beating, while King's followers conducted themselves with firmness yet restraint. During the marches of his era, he asked his followers not to retaliate. Even when his own home and family were bombed, he *spoke* furiously, but *acted* gently. In a sermon the night before his assassination, he said:

> *There's talk about what might happen to me from some of our sick white brothers ... But it doesn't matter to me now, because I've been to the mountain top! ... Like anybody I'd like to live a long life. Longevity has its place. But I'm not concerned about that now ... He's allowed me to go up the mountain! and I've looked over, and I've seen the promised land! I may not get there with you, but I want you to know tonight ... that we, as a people, will get to the promised land! And I'm happy tonight. I'm not worried about anything. I'm not fearing any man! Mine eyes have seen the glory of the coming of the Lord!* (from King's Memphis sermon, quoted in Hampden-Turner, 1981, p. 207)

King's life personified dynamic forgiveness. He was not complacent or compromising, yet describing potential assassins as *brothers* is surely reminiscent of One whose dying words were "Father, forgive them ..."

In this chapter we've seen how a sense of "alien dignity" stabilizes our self-esteem and provides a family system which enables us to treat other humans as sisters and brothers, worthy of our love and forgiveness. In the next chapter we'll learn how our philosophy of personal freedom or determinism subconsciously determines whether we will blame or forgive others.

Chapter 2

How *Circumstances* Color Forgiveness

*In the late afternoon of January 13, 1982, during a blind-
ing snowstorm, Air Florida Flight 90 from Washington,
D.C. to Tampa and Fort Lauderdale crashed into the
Fourteenth Street Bridge just seconds after taking off from
National Airport. The airplane had undergone de-icing
procedures 45 minutes before take-off, but lumbered down
the airport's 6,870-foot runway, failed to gain altitude,
struck the bridge crowded with rush-hour traffic, and
plunged into the iced-over waters of the Potomac River.
Upon impact the tail section of the plane separated from
the main portion of the fuselage, and this forward part of
the aircraft quickly sank in the river. Only five of the 79
people aboard the plane were rescued; an additional four
people were killed who had been traveling across the
bridge at the time of impact.* (Shaver, 1985, p. 11)

A plane crash always raises many questions. Had the de-icing
procedures been properly performed? Did too much time elapse
between de-icing and take-off? Were the pilots accustomed to fly-
ing in wintry conditions? Did they carefully consider the risks, or
were they more concerned with regaining time lost waiting to take
off than with weather conditions? Should airport officials have
closed the runways earlier in the day? Was the flight path — chosen in compliance with noise-abatement regulations and requiring
an immediate turn to follow the river — intrinsically unsafe? Is the
runway at National simply too short? Are the de-icing systems of a
Boeing 737 adequate for storm conditions? Were other systems on
the plane working properly? Were control tower personnel adequately trained to evaluate such conditions? Could a terrorist have
planted a bomb?

These and numerous other "What-caused-this-crash?" queries invariably follow a disaster of this kind. Experts from the National Transportation Safety Board typically spend weeks or months sifting through debris, questioning witnesses, listening to the flight recorder, and generally gathering as much information as they can to determine what went wrong.

But, you ask, what has this got to do with forgiveness? Plenty. Because steering your behavior is much like piloting an airplane. Scores of variables funnel into your final stream of action, and if your behavior "crashes," causing injury to others or yourself, people will speculate as to "Why?" You won't be confronted with investigators from the National Transportation Safety Board, but your church board or the school board, your spouse, children, or friends will likely ask, "What happened? What went wrong?"

How you answer such questions will powerfully influence how easily you forgive. Most people find it easy to pardon people for things they can't help, but enormously difficult to excuse people when they conclude, "They should have known better!"

Many religious people find themselves in a catch-22 when it comes to freedom of choice and forgiveness. They believe that people have freedom of choice — they *decide* to follow a certain course of behavior. Consequently, they are *responsible* for the outcomes of their behavior. Yet such a belief makes it hard to dispense forgiveness because when someone messes up, we're likely to say to ourselves, "They knew better!" Or, "They *chose* to do that, so now they have to suffer the consequences." In popular jargon: "They made their bed; now they've got to sleep in it."

In this chapter we'll consider some fundamental psychological and philosophical questions: What is behavior? Do people *choose* how to act, or is behavior decided by factors in the environment? Do I steer my behavior, or am I a product of my upbringing with little choice? What causes behavior? What is an event? Such questions may seem either trivial or intimidating, but please stay with me, because these issues are important ingredients in our understanding of forgiveness.

Behavior: Inside-Out Or Outside-In?

Asking "What is behavior?" might seem as ridiculous as the esoteric philosopher asking "What is a chair?" or "Does this table really exist?" It seems obvious that behaving is simply how people act, what they do. Further, most of us grow up thinking that behavior moves inside-out, that it flows from somewhere deep within — like lava emerging from a volcanic mountain, originating at an inner source known as personality. We believe that somewhere deep inside the brain's central command center, personality directs traffic much as an air traffic controller guides incoming and outgoing flights. Most of us feel that we personally direct our behavior from a "command center" deep inside ourselves. This inside-out (I call it the volcano model) flow of behavior makes perfect sense and is widely popular.

But some psychologists, like the late behaviorist B. F. Skinner, champion an outside-in (I call it the moon-tide model) perspective. They insist that human beings exert little steermanship over their lives, and that people are pushed and pulled about by external rewards and punishments, much as the moon exerts a pull on ocean waters creating tides. For Skinner and other behaviorists, such external influences are much more powerful in determining the course of behavior than are "willpower" or the "inner self."

Placing their primary emphasis on the **external situation**, behaviorists argue that the consistency seen in behavior is not so much a function of inner goals, motives, or drives, but rather results from "consistent" situational demands. For example, the reason you don't tell jokes at funerals has more to do with the external situation than with your inner sense of humor. The reason your heart beats more briskly when a police officer stops you for speeding has more to do with your circumstances than your cardiac fitness. In such instances your behavior is primarily shaped by what's happening outside yourself, just as ocean tides are created by the outside gravitational forces of the moon acting on the water. In the extreme case, behaviorists argue that *all* behavior is shaped by external forces. An early behaviorist, J. B. Watson, put it this way:

Give me a dozen healthy infants, well-formed, and my own specified world to bring them up in and I'll guarantee to take any one at random and train him to become any type of specialist I might select — doctor, lawyer, artist, merchant, chief, and yes, even beggarman and thief, regardless of his talents, penchants, tendencies, abilities, vocations, and race of his ancestors. (1924, p. 82)

Other psychologists (psychoanalysts, client-centered, humanistic, existential, and so forth — the "self" psychologists) emphasize the **inner** person. For them freedom is found in the *self choosing* to do or not do certain things. They argue that we are able to *transcend* the situation — by sometimes *choosing* to go against the current — by defying the odds and *deciding* our own destinies.

Self (inside-out) psychologists have typically faced off against behavioristic (outside-in) psychologists, with the former arguing for central direction and control and the latter insisting on the primacy of circumstances.

Behavior As Dynamic Interaction

As is the case in so many antipodal arguments, these two viewpoints define the extremes of a continuum, with truth residing somewhere in the middle. In fact, behavior isn't *totally* driven by circumstances, nor is it *completely* inner-directed. More importantly, asking "*which is it?*" becomes the wrong question, because it suggests there is a single correct answer. In fact, the true answer is *both*. Behavior is influenced *both* by inner forces and external circumstances.

Among psychologists this is known as the **interactional** perspective, and it is the one I will utilize in this book. I believe that behavior is *both* inside-out *and* outside-in. Furthermore, viewing behavior as *either* the product of a person *or* the result of the situation is lopsided. I hope to show that *behavior is a dynamic interaction between persons and the situations in which they find themselves — not the sole product of either.* Another way of saying this is that persons *and* situations *both* influence behavior. *Self and situation both drive behavior.* The question, "Is behavior caused by

28

the person *or* the situation?" is meaningless. Better to ask "*How do persons and situations interact?*"

Similarly, freedom and determinism have been often been pitted against each other as opposite "things." Hard-line behaviorists (like J. B. Watson or B. F. Skinner) make it seem as if the situation *totally* shapes the individual's behavior. Other psychologists argue that forces *within* the person produce growth ("self-actualization") often *in spite of* what is in the environment.

Once we begin to understand that persons and situations are inseparably interwoven in continuously flowing behavior, the clash between freedom and determinism no longer makes sense. Typically freedom of choice has been pictured as the sole domain of the person, under constant attack by forces in the environment, seeking to lead the unsuspecting person into forbidden paths. But picturing inner freedom as fighting against situational determinism is misleading. When we understand behavior to be **interactional**, we see that freedom and determinism are like two dancers — complementarily intertwined, playing off one another, both necessary to the process. Now let's look at each of these dancers — freedom and determinism.

Freedom comes in many varieties. In everyday conversation we use "freedom" in widely differing ways. Sociopolitically it can mean opportunities *to do* certain things, such as vote, seek public office, or sit in the front of a bus without fear. Freedom can also mean liberty to *not do* certain onerous tasks. People who win the lottery often quit their jobs and, "free" from the need to earn a living through daily toil, buy a motor home, travel, take up golf, or dabble in watercolors. Freedom sometimes means *release from* external forces that feel confining, coercing, imprisoning, and the like. Indeed, the goal of parents is to rear children who grow up replacing external parental control with *internal* self-control. Here freedom amounts to developing an interior life capable of suitably managing emotions.

Freedom And Forgiveness

Notice now how these two differing views tilt your inclination to forgive. If you believe that self steers behavior, you will attribute

29

a high degree of choice to the person and correspondingly a high degree of *responsibility*. Subconsciously this will make you much *less* forgiving and *more* blaming when such a person errs. Many religious people are prone to this view and are subsequently quick to hold people "responsible" (which usually means "to blame") when behavior "crashes."

By contrast, if you believe that people are a product of conditioning, shaped by the environment, you'll not see them as having much freedom, but neither will you be likely to blame them when things don't turn out well. Indeed, B. F. Skinner, this century's leading proponent of behaviorism, suggested that "freedom" and "dignity" were illusions, based on the erroneous idea that people actually steer their own behavior. Behaviorists have argued that there are no good or bad people, just good or bad environments.

It's not hard to see why such assertions are anathema to moralists and clergy. If such an assertion were accepted as completely true, it would, in a single *coup de grace,* wipe out centuries of moral structures painstakingly built on the bedrock of personal responsibility. Theologians, philosophers, and clergymen understand this clearly. They know that confession, forgiveness, pardon, penance, and other related religious concepts help to expunge the believer's guilt over wrongdoing. But they also know that guilt must be firmly anchored on the bedrock of free will, choice, and personal responsibility.

Freedom And Determinism Are Complementary

As you might guess by now, the surprising solution is that **freedom and determinism co-exist**. In Chinese philosophy Yin and Yang symbolize the timeless ebb and flow in all of nature, a rhythmic movement among opposites, two sides of the same mountain. Similarly, freedom and determinism are two inseparable sides of the behavioral process.

If there were no stable external boundaries in a situation, you couldn't *choose* to behave consistently. Freedom to choose among options assumes that the options will remain stable. You can't win a football game if the goalposts move every time the ball is passed. You can't decide whether the baseball hurled in your direction by the pitcher will be called a strike or a ball if home plate moves while the pitch is en route! This complementarity is clearly stated in the following words:

> *Being the product of conditioning and being free to change do not war with each other. Both are true. They coexist ... We must affirm freedom and responsibility without denying that we are the product of circumstance, and we must affirm that we are the product of circumstance without denying that we have the freedom to transcend that causality to become something which could not have been previsioned from the circumstances which shaped us.* (Wheelis, 1973, pp. 87, 88)

We must respect and guard the balance between freedom and determinism, because either extreme is dangerous. At one extreme B. F. Skinner argued that freedom is an illusion; we are simply a complex mass of conditioned responses. At the opposite extreme, Werner Erhard, founder of EST, argues that everything that happens to you happens because you choose it. Both Skinner and Erhard are *partially* right, but in their extremism both become dreadfully wrong. Rollo May captured the balance nicely in the following words:

> *I propose that **freedom and determinism give birth to each other. Every advance in freedom gives birth to a new determinism, and every new determinism gives birth in its turn to new freedom.** Freedom is a circle within a larger circle of determinism. This goes on progressively into infinity. The function of the self in this picture can be seen by a simple analogy of dropping a stone in a still lake, **the self is the center as the experiencing agent.** In this sense, the centered self continuously takes into itself both freedom and determinism; it is a process bounded only by infinity.*
> *By refusing to accept either determinism or freedom, we diminish ourselves. Without determinism, and the predictability that goes with it, we have* anarchy. *Without freedom, and the exuberance that goes with it, we have* apathy. (May, 1977)

Self And Situation — Twin Determinants Of Behavior

Persons and situations are inseparable and we are *partially* shaped by our situation, and *partially* directed by our inner self. We must now tackle the problem of determining how much freedom we have in a specific situation. First, however, we need to understand the statistical term **degrees of freedom**.

Statisticians carefully account for how many alternatives are available before assigning probabilities. Thus, a tossed coin has only two "choices" of how to land — heads or tails, whereas a cube has six. Statistically, we say that tossing a coin has fewer **degrees of freedom** than rolling dice. The same is true of complex behaviors such as choosing a restaurant for dinner. A "going-out-to-dinner" event has more degrees of freedom in Chicago or Atlanta than in Kalamazoo. Wheelchair users have fewer degrees of freedom in escaping a burning building than their able-bodied counterparts. A karate instructor has more degrees of freedom in warding off a mugger than I do. You get the idea.

Degrees of freedom helps to sort out the freedom-determinism dilemma. For any particular behavior, we can assume the person has *partial* choice (*some* degrees of freedom). But we must quickly acknowledge that such "freedom" is never total — the self has limited *degrees* of freedom to steer behavior. Similarly, the *situation* always contributes significantly to the outcome — again a certain *degree* of influence. Furthermore, this is seldom a 50-50 split with self and situation evenly "responsible" for the outcome. In many cases it may be 75-25 or even 90-10. How much self contributes and how much the situation contributes varies from event to event.

Now we come to an important conclusion: **Freedom brings responsibility (and blame)**. The more degrees of freedom we assign to the person, the more likely we are to blame, and conversely less likely to forgive. If, on the other hand, we allocate most of the degrees of freedom to the situation instead of the person we are far less likely to blame the person.

Imagine I'm traveling on a crowded subway when a large man steps on my toe or roughly brushes against me in a way that causes me to drop the book I'm holding. I angrily think of numerous

32

alternatives (assigning him numerous degrees of freedom): "He ought to watch where he's going!" "Why aren't people more careful?" "Whatever happened to common courtesy?" "Why are people always in a hurry?" "At the very least, he could apologize once he's seen what happened!" I would hold him highly responsible — I would blame.

Now picture for a moment that I'm about to say, "Hey! Watch where you're going!" or in some other way forcefully confront this rude person with his behavior. But just as I'm about to speak, I notice he's holding a white cane and wearing dark glasses — even though it's evening. Instantly I re-assign degrees of freedom. At once my anger changes to chagrin — "I almost yelled at a blind man!" This happens automatically, instantly, powerfully.

Most of us would do well to cultivate consciously an appreciation for the *complexity* of *situations*, because we generally apportion too many degrees of freedom to people, and too few to situations. When we begin to comprehend how many possible *situational* factors influence behavior, we will be less likely to hold others so *totally* responsible for their behaviors. Then it will become easier to forgive.

To return to our original example, figuring out whom to blame when a plane crashes is a very complicated process, but we seldom realize that *steering personal behavior is more complex than piloting a plane*! And since psychological sciences are not as well developed as physics and engineering, it's usually impossible to be completely certain why a particular behavior "crashes." Let me close by raising a final question. It's one of those questions to which the answer, at first glance, seems so obvious as to hardly be worth asking. But like the other questions we've asked, it illustrates the complexity that resides just beneath the surface of the "ordinary."

What Is An Event?

We've seen that when a plane crashes it becomes difficult to precisely locate *the cause*. Deciding whether to attribute the crash to situational factors or internal causes like "pilot error" is not easy, and it always turns out that there are *multiple causes*.

We've seen how complicated it becomes to clearly locate a "cause." Often, however, in everyday life, it is difficult even to define what is an "event." In the case of an airplane crashing or some behavioral disaster such as a murder, the focal event seems rather clear, but in the case of "ordinary" everyday events it is not always clear.

Shaver (1985) examines the complexity of the commonplace by discussing what happens if he burns a pile of leaves:

> Suppose that I am spending a windy fall afternoon burning a pile of leaves that I have collected from my yard. What is "the event"? It is certainly true that I am (a) "burning leaves," but I may also be (b) "preparing for winter." My neighbors downwind would notice that I am (c) "filling the house up with smoke," and they might believe I am also (d) "recklessly endangering the dry woods" behind both our houses. If there is a county ordinance against open fires before 4:00 p.m, then I am also (e) "breaking the law." The action is (f) "contributing particulate matter to the air" and quite possibly (g) "increasing the discomfort of sufferers from emphysema." Finally, if it is a weekday afternoon, I am also (h) "being unavailable to students." Even simple actions can have multiple, often simultaneous, effects, and any combinations of these can be used to define "the event." (1985, p. 40)

I hope you now appreciate how complex is the process of clearly defining "causes" and "events." Yet we all engage in this kind of analysis every day — moment by moment — hardly aware of how profoundly it influences our response to others. Shaver discusses differing responses to his leaf burning:

> Someone who considered me merely to be burning leaves would not be likely to take any action. By contrast, a perceiver who considered me to be breaking the law, endangering the woods, or polluting the air might very well call the authorities. But even in this case, **which** authorities were notified — police, firefighters, or the clean air agency — would depend on the particular description of the event. (1985, p. 40)

In our present discussion this means that when I burn leaves, whether my neighbor enjoys the aroma of burning leaves and "**forgives**" me for filling her house with smoke, or whether she becomes angry and upset and summons the sheriff, depends on how she perceives "causes" and "events," and her personal history with regard to autumn.

Blame, Responsibility, And Forgiveness

Forgiveness is closely related to blame. If you don't blame, there's nothing to forgive. But more importantly, *how* you blame will affect *how* you forgive. It is probably obvious that we *blame* only when something goes wrong, when there's a disaster. We never "blame" a musician for performing a difficult violin concerto with ease and splendor. We don't **blame** a speaker for entertaining us with lively stories. It's only when the violin string breaks or the speaker bores us to sleep that we look around for what or whom to blame. We've seen, however, that this is not a simple process. In fact it becomes almost impossible ever to find *the* cause, *the* event, or correctly ascertain *the* motives of the person participating in the event — even so simple an event as burning leaves!

We must conclude that *it is extremely difficult to blame accurately*, because we must first establish what happened and then assign blame correctly. At lower levels of complexity, it appears that we can establish causes and effects (the cue ball hit the eight ball, driving it into the corner pocket, or the face of the three wood squarely contacted the golf ball, driving it down the fairway), but most "ordinary" behaviors involve **multiple levels** of cause-effect chains inextricably intertwined, and your analysis will be influenced by the level at which you try to understand.

Even such a "simple" act as searching for a paper clip in my desk drawer can be described in terms of precise muscle movements of my fingers, arms, and limbs; or in more global terms behaviors such as opening or closing drawers; or finally in terms of the action as a whole. But this entire "fluid system" is involved and the answer to "What are you doing?" can be answered at many different levels. Such complexity may seem overwhelming, but we can extricate ourselves by realizing that it is much like a spiral stairway with many landings. We can choose to stop, catch our breath, and contemplate at any level we desire. It isn't always necessary — or possible — to climb all the stairs, but we *must* appreciate the complexity of the superstructure.

It seems apparent that we seldom have enough information to decipher accurately someone else's personal liability in a given situation. Which means we ought to err on the side of forgiving rather than blaming.

Separating **blame** and **responsibility** is an important ethical priority. I would like to make a crucial statement: **It is possible to be partially responsible for conditions in other people's lives — indeed even to have contributed to the aggregate of causes that led to a certain consequence — without being blameworthy.** This is the pivotal point of this chapter. We've seen how complex are the networks of causes, events, and motives that shape our behaviors. It's possible to examine such things *without blaming* — heredity, parents, peers, or God. An awareness of complexity ought to make us less blaming and more forgiving. Instead of seeking whom to blame, we might study the complexity of a particular "crash" and think of how this might be prevented in the future; without necessarily blaming the pilot, control tower, or de-icing equipment, we might implement improvements in all the suspected areas. We could institute better pilot training, more extensive control tower instruction, and study ways to improve de-icing equipment.

We must also recognize, however, that blaming (euphemistically — "holding *others* responsible") is at the core of being human. Whenever something goes wrong, we naturally seek to distance ourselves from it by locating it somewhere outside ourselves. In the earliest social psychology on record we find the blaming process at work. The perfect garden of Eden (*situation*) is disrupted by the disaster of disobedience, and Adam seeks to transfer the guilt and discomfort from his *inner self* to something *out there*. When God questions Adam, the blame chain begins:

> ... *"Have you eaten from the tree that I commanded you not to eat from?"*

36

> *The man said, "The **woman you** put here with me —*
> *she gave me some fruit from the tree, and I ate it."*
> *Then the Lord God said to the woman, "What is this*
> *you have done?"*
> *The woman said, "**The serpent** deceived me and I ate."*
> (Genesis 3:11-13, bold face mine)

The woman, the serpent, God — who cares? Just get rid of the discomfort — place it outside yourself! *Blame* someone or something *out there*!

Toddlers, Theology And Luck

In summary, we must accept blaming — like breathing — as a normal part of our humanity, but quickly add that forgiveness is an opportunity to transcend the smallness of our egocentricity. The phrase "To err is human, to forgive is divine" misses the crucial point. We humans **can** at times transcend our errors — even the errors of others — and forgive. To err is human, but so is forgiveness. God doesn't have a monopoly on forgiveness.

Indeed, God expects me to grow beyond the tininess of toddler thinking and understand that when you knocked over my stack of blocks, you might not have done it on purpose. Your degrees of freedom were limited by the fact that, having just recently learned to walk, you were losing your balance and about to fall on your face. Now, as an adult, you have no trouble walking, but you made mistakes in your work because you were distracted by news you had recently received that a close friend is dying of a terminal illness. As an adult, I am capable of carrying out such analyses, and my forgiveness ought to keep pace.

Toddler understandings lead to toddler forgiveness. Most parents have engaged in trying to "teach toddlers forgiveness" in the following way:

> *Parent:(with stern resolve) "Jimmy, now that you've*
> *quit hitting Sean, I want you to tell him you're sorry!"*
> *Jimmy: (scowling) ... [silence]*
> *Parent: (flushed with "resolve") "Go ahead!"*
> *Jimmy: (defiantly) ... [silence]*

37

> *Parent:* *"OK, Jimmy if that's how you're going to be, you'll sit in the corner — and no TV — until you're sorry."*
> *[Sean, of course, makes no attempt to mask his delight.]*

Much later —

> *Parent: (with relief)* *"OK, I see you're ready now. Jimmy, go ahead."*
> *Jimmy: (contemptuously)* *"I'm sorry."*
> *Parent: (sternly, again)* *"Say it like you mean it!"*
> *Jimmy: (only slightly less contemptuously)* *"I'm sorry!"*
> *Parent: (with relief)* *"OK now, Sean, I want you to for-give Jimmy. He said he was sorry, now what do you say?"*
> *Sean: (appearing puzzled)* ... *"Dunno."*
> *Parent: (with resolve)* *"You say 'I'm sorry too.' "*
> *Sean: (defiantly)* ... *[silence]*
> *Parent: (trying to maintain patience)* *"Go ahead! ..."*

You get the picture. Such cycles are tiring to parents, trying to toddlers, and often leave everyone feeling irritated. I hope that our preceding discussion will help you replace the forgiveness rituals of childhood with the understandings of adult life.

I've concluded that it is nearly impossible for me to determine how many degrees of freedom you have when you behave in a particular way. I ought to be open to giving you the benefit of the doubt — and there is always plenty of doubt to spread around. I can safely assume that you were influenced by forces from within *and* forces from without.

Finally, I think we need to temper our theology with *luck*. Shaver reminds us that many disasters occur without human causality:

> *Many causes can exist independent of intervention by human beings — tornadoes cause extensive damage, bacteria cause disease in animals, lengthening spring days cause new leaves to appear on trees — so the actions of persons constitute **only a fraction of the antecedents of effects**.* (1985, p. 87, bold face mine)

The wise man reminds us that luck is always a part of the equation:

I have seen something else under the sun:
The race is not to the swift
  or the battle to the strong,
nor does food come to the wise
  or wealth to the brilliant
  or favor to the learned;
*but time and **chance** happen to them all.*
(Ecclesiastes 9:11, bold face mine)

It's impossible for me to assess how much "ice on your wings" was produced by the "coldness" of your of work associates. I can never be exactly certain what you were thinking, because the "flight recorder" of your thoughts can't be recovered without distortion. I don't know what the "weather conditions" of your family life were at the moment. I don't know how well your "flight instructors" (parents) prepared you to deal with emergencies. I don't have adequate specs regarding the structural integrity of your "Boeing 737" (body), and I'm not sure whether all systems were operating at the time of takeoff.

Given the bewildering complexity of your situation and the impossibility of assessing your degrees of freedom, I'll lean toward forgiveness. Rather than arrogantly presume "You made the choice!" I'll assume that many factors were operating over which you had no control and to which I am not privy. Since I have incomplete information, I'll not judge how responsible you are, and unless called for jury duty, I'll spend my free time trying to figure out how to pilot my own plane a bit more smoothly.

Too often I've used the phrase *"If I were you ..."* followed with advice about how you ought to solve your problems. Trouble is, I'm *not* you. Taking all this into account, I now have less advice to offer, because the fact is *If I were you ... I would do exactly what you are now doing*!

In this chapter we've seen how complex is the process of understanding human behavior. We've also seen how profoundly our personal philosophy influences our world view, even if we are not

39

aware of it — especially when we're not aware of it! I hope our understanding of the complexity of situations will help us not only to forgive, but to forgive a bit more easily.

I've tried to acquaint you with a few of the many **outside** influences that shape your behavior. We've looked from the "outside-in" or **objective** perspective; next we'll look from the "inside-out" or **subjective** viewpoint. You'll find this easier to digest, because it's where you experience life each moment of the day. That's why it's sometimes referred to as **experiential psychology.** In the next few chapters we'll be using the concept of psychological **style** to talk about **consistency** of behavior which comes from within the person. Stay tuned.

Chapter 3

How *Personality Styles* Influence Forgiveness

(Histrionic Style)

Next, I want to help you understand how your inner life — your personality style — influences forgiveness. Each of us has a unique personality — unique software — for processing and relating to the world around us. Thirty years ago, when I first began teaching abnormal psychology to university students, I often found myself involved in after-class discussions that went something like this:

"Dr. Berecz, I like to keep all the things on my desk in order, and I sometimes 'check' things several times. Do you think I'm an obsessive-compulsive?"

"Probably not," I would reply. "You see, *real* obsessive-compulsives have an inflexible urge for fastidiousness. You might prefer to have a neat desk, but I suspect that it's not really a compulsion."

Then I would spend the next few minutes circumspectly dancing around the issue, assuring the anxious student that he/she was very different from "patients" whom I treated in my private practice. Then, as I drove across town to do psychotherapy with "real" patients, I would wonder if I had adequately reassured the student; or I would plan how to make the distinction between patients and normal people more clear in my next lecture.

Now, three decades later, I realize I was wrong, and now my after-class discussions are brief, and more accurate:

"Dr. Berecz, I keep all the pencils on my desk in a row ... do you think I'm obsessive-compulsive?"

"Probably." Then, for reassurance: "We all are."

Then I explain, as I'm about to explain to you, that the differences between us (the "normal" ones) and them (the "patients") is

41

mostly a matter of degrees. The same sorts of predicaments that bring people into my office to lie on my leather couch or sit in my overstuffed chair for fifty minutes of psychotherapy are similar to problems encountered by everyone; more profound, perhaps, but similar. Even patients requiring hospitalization are more similar to you and me than we usually imagine.

In the next two chapters I'll discuss psychological styles in order to help you understand how styles influence forgiveness. I'll examine two styles — histrionic and obsessive-compulsive — in depth and briefly consider how such people give and receive forgiveness. I'd like to start by introducing you to Monique.

Histrionic Style

Monique

Reverend Jim slouched into the dark green chair behind his desk. Closing his eyes, he allowed the soft leather to caress his body with its inherent TLC. He even permitted himself the luxury of some self-pity. "Why do I always have to be on the giving end of the guidance process?" he wearily wondered. It doesn't always feel "more blessed" to give than to receive! Three o'clock in the afternoon is a flat time anyway. Late enough in the day to feel tired but too early to quit. Besides, tomorrow's sermon really needed a few finishing touches.

The phone annoyingly interrupted Jim's reverie.

"Reverend!" It was Monique. "I've got to talk to you right away!"

Her voice, always breathy with emotion, was unmistakable. Jim knew her — everyone in the church did! — but he'd never seen her for counseling before.

Monique was his newest parishioner, having been converted during a recent revival series. She'd been the first one to come forward at the altar call. Her enthusiasm for her newfound faith was contagious and her effervescent witnessing, with its animated detailing of her "Before-I-found-Jesus" life provided a colorful narrative that held teenagers' attention better than Nintendo.

Monique seemed to experience everything in the present moment, and when she recounted past sins and riotous living it was as if she were re-living — more than recalling — her past mistakes. Once, barely a week after joining Pastor Jim's parish, she had scandalized the congregation with her vivid testimony, animatedly reminiscing of how "horrific" her life had been before finding Jesus and how "fantabulous" it was now. As she soared to new heights of emotion, her passionate crescendo was no doubt facilitated by the enthusiastic adoration of the assembled members who expressed their approval in fervent responses. "Praise the Lord!" "Amen!" "Glory be!" At the dizzying pinnacle of this heart-stirring progression Monique half wept and half shouted: "And since I found Jesus Christ as my personal Savior, I've never been so ****ing happy in all my life!"

Reverend Jim, who had been on the platform that evening, couldn't help grimacing, even now, as he recalled the looks of horror that crossed the faces of some of the antique saints and the irrepressible laughter that erupted from the adolescent and young adult crowd. Whatever else Monique was, she was unforgettable. Recently however, the parish was awash in rumors that her "changed" life was reverting to the "before" state that she was so gifted in describing.

Jim's musings were aborted by the sounds of giggling and laughter in the reception area. Monique had arrived! She never just arrived, it was always an "entrance." Now as she draped herself across his office couch, Pastor Jim was reminded that there was always a seductive edge to everything Monique did. It was apparent even in the choice of her name. Though her baptismal certificate read "Monica" she had not used her given name in years. She once explained to Pastor Jim.

"Monica is what my parents named me, but I thought it was boring, so when I started a new school in the seventh grade I told everyone my name was Monique! (giggle) It sounded French! Sexy!"

Jim could picture it. Monique, the sexy seventh grader! Though she was now 34, her emotional experience seemed more adolescent than adult. Her personality was a puzzling blend of I-want-you-to-hold-me needy little girl and I've-got-to-have-you sensuous woman. Men found the combination compelling; women despised her.

Wrinkles were discernible at the outside edges of her eyelids, though her heavy makeup all but obliterated them. When she giggled — which was often enough to provide punctuation for her sentences — the corners of her mouth created noticeable smile wrinkles. Her breathy, theatrical voice had a contrived quality which was rendered the more incongruous by her giggle-while-you-talk nervousness and her caricaturely-applied lipstick and mascara. She almost looked like a streetwalker. The neon lettering on her tightly stretched black T-shirt screamed "Heavy Metal Forever" competing with a large yellow happy-faced "Smile God Loves You" button strategically nestled between her ample breasts. Her miniskirt barely covered her thighs. If one word could summarize her appearance it was *incongruous*.

Monique appeared waiflike yet streetwise, childlike but sexual, exhibitionistic yet bashful, independent while hungry for attention. Though she was sexually provocative, her femininity lacked depth. She seemed like a twelve-year-old playing grown-up — trying to dress like a sexy 34-year-old, but not knowing how. She began, as Monique always did, by making direct contact:

"What should I call you? 'Reverend?' or 'Jim?' " she asked.

"What would you like to call me?" responded the pastor.

"Gosh! I'm not sure. (giggles) 'Reverend' seems spooky. I've always been scared of preachers." (breathy laughter)

"Well, suppose you call me 'Pastor Jim.' Does that seem less scary?"

"I guess! Well, Geeminee! You're the boss! ... Right? (giggle) It's just this place seems so spooky!"

"Spooky?" said Jim.

(giggle) "Yeah, you know, you've got this big green leather couch, and that chair you sit in looks like the one shrinks use in movies. (giggle) I always wondered what it would be like to go to 'confession' so now I'm here."

Pastor Jim briefly reminded her that as a Protestant pastor, he didn't conduct "confessionals," but she seemed hardly to listen and continued nonetheless to confess:

"You're a marriage counselor, right? Well, gee whiz! I don't exactly know just how to say this, so I guess I'll just blurt it out ..." (lots of giggling)

44

"Go ahead," Pastor Jim quietly encouraged. "I'm listening."

"Golly! Uh, I don't have orgasms — at least I don't think I do. But I give great oral sex. At least that's what Tom says (more giggles) ... I mean, he never complains!"

Her incessant chatter stopped for the moment and she paused as her tongue sensuously traced the inside of her slightly pursed lips. She was enjoying Pastor Jim's attention and carried out this subtle oral maneuver with the skill of an experienced striptease artist.

"I guess maybe I try to make up for the fact that I don't have orgasms by giving him the best time he's ever had in other ways! — If you know what I mean!"

They were less than five minutes into their meeting and Monique was animatedly expounding her skills at oral sex as if she were speaking of baking chocolate chip cookies.

In the visits that followed, little changed. The only thing predictable about Monique's life was that her consistently outrageous behavior generated continual chaos around her. She didn't feel anxious, guilty, remorseful, or depressed, like some of Jim's other parishioners; rather, any brief negative feelings were immediately swamped — flooded — by the emotional intensity of the moment.

Although Jim didn't feel his efforts to help her develop spiritual insight met with much success, he continued counseling her for several months. It seemed to provide a measure of coherence to her turbulent life. Although she never stayed with any topic long enough to examine it in depth, she did occasionally ask his advice about a specific problem (like whether or not she should quit working part-time at a topless bar) and then would follow his suggestions.

One of the challenges of working with such intensely emotional individuals (usually diagnosed as **histrionic** personalities) is that they are so dominated by feelings that their thoughts seem to have little influence over their lives. For instance, Monique once showed up for a counseling session in an exceptionally excited mood. The atmosphere of the office crackled with the electricity of her excitement:

45

"O-o-o-o-o-h, Pastor Jim," she excitedly stammered as she tried to clear a path through her mental jumble. "I needed to see you right away!"

Her pupils dilated with eagerness, her body quivered with excitement. "I ... I ... just *had* to see you *today*," she continued, "because our last session was the most important thing that's ever happened in my life! It *totally* changed how I see things! It's like I'm a new person! I'll *never* be the same again. Your counseling is really fantabulous! I'm a *completely* changed person."

Although by now Jim had become somewhat accustomed to Monique's emotional exaggerations, this time he felt like something remarkable really had occurred. He searched his memory of their last session but couldn't come up with anything extraordinary. Meanwhile, Monique seemed to have slipped into an uncharacteristic contemplative silence.

"Please," Pastor Jim encouraged her, "go on ... tell me what had such an impact on you last session?"

"But that's just it ..."

Monique's voice trailed off, and Jim thought he noticed tears moistening her eyes.

"That's why I *had* to come today," she murmured plaintively, *"I can't remember what we talked about!"*

***

Such is the mind of the hysteric. Dominated by **impressions**, lacking details, overwhelmed with emotions, such persons seem incapable of measured, considered, judgment. Captivated by the flashy, the emotional, the exciting, they appear incapable of careful analytic thinking. When you're with a histrionic person, you often feel like you're surfing on an emotional tidal wave.

Before examining the histrionic style in more depth, let's take a moment to define **style**.

> *Suppose we observe an Indian, whose culture is unfamiliar, performing a strange dance with great intensity. As we watch, puzzled, we may notice that there is a drought and that this is an agricultural community; we consider*

the possibility that this is a prayerful dance designed to bring rain ... But the limitations of that understanding become apparent if we only consider that nearby, watching, is a non-Indian farmer who also suffers from the drought but does not join in the dancing. It does not occur to him to perform these gestures; instead, he goes home and worries. **The Indian dances not only because there is a drought, but also because he is an Indian.** (Shapiro, 1965, p. 16)

In the previous chapter we focused on the many ways in which external **situations** shape behavior, now we will consider those **inner consistencies** which "make an Indian uniquely an Indian." We'll refer to this inner consistency as **style**, and we'll try to walk in the Indian's moccasins in order to understand his personal inner world. And, as you might guess, forgiveness is shaped by the style or personality of the person providing the forgiveness.

Personality Style

Style refers to those **consistent behaviors** that seem to emerge within yourself. Style is what you think of as your **personality**. It refers to behaviors that are personally and uniquely "You." Style captures the consistencies of behavior without making it sound like you are cast in concrete.

Remember your last high school reunion? You likely noticed changes in your classmates — receding hairlines, sagging bustlines, expanding waistlines — but somehow their inner selves survived the ravages of time better than their bodies. Their psychological styles seemed — like those quick-frozen hairy mammoths — preserved essentially unchanged. The class clown is still the life of the party, the loudmouth can be still be heard above the rest. The class siren is now a flirtatious middle-ager, and the jocks are placing bets on the Super Bowl. You experience *deja vu* because style resists change, and if you attend another reunion in five or ten years, you'll still recognize everyone. It's a little like watching a *Thirty Years of Johnny Carson* special.

Since we find individuality among the flowers, trees, and fish, it shouldn't surprise us that in the zenith of God's creation —

humankind — uniqueness abounds. People, like snowflakes and fingerprints, are distinctively individual. Even "identical" twins are not really identical! Nonetheless, alongside each person's uniqueness, we find **consistencies** of behavior and **general similarities** to others. We refer to these consistencies as **style**.

Within seconds or minutes of being with Monique-style people, you notice how **impressionistic** they are. They live in a world of **feelings** barely touched by thinking. They are drawn to the dramatic — to whatever excites feelings. They are the headline readers of the news, channel-flipping soap-and-talk-show viewers of television, and, if they read at all, Harlequin devotees. While other people *search* for things in the world — ideas, goals, meaning — or *create* careers, families, or causes, the "Moniques" are *struck* by things. They travel through life flamboyantly and bombastically, but passively. Victims more often than perpetrators, their shallowness of thought and hunger for excitement make them prey for a variety of more calculating exploitive persons.

Histrionic women seem, at first glance, to be "oversexed." Erotically provocative, coquettish, and coy, they engage in cat-and-mouse flirtations with members of the opposite sex. Such behaviors are in evidence not only during culturally-sanctioned occasions such as the office Christmas party, but occur in virtually all situations including grocery stores, banks, and work settings. Such women are sensuously provocative in dress, cosmetics, posture, and attitudes. More generally, they are exhibitionistic about almost everything — including medical problems, physical defects, psychological needs, and religious experience.

Colored by Culture. It needs to be noted that all styles are shaped by the culture and the times. Indeed, the gracefully fainting ladies of the Victorian period were given "permission" by their cultures to perfect "swooning" into a socially-acceptable skill. Today, due to changed cultural conditions, such dramatics are unacceptable, and consequently the histrionic skill of fainting gracefully has all but disappeared.

Society conditions male histrionics to express themselves differently than females. Instead of manifesting their dependency needs through helplessness or frailty as is often seen with females, they are more likely to seek soothing through alcohol or drugs. Frequently such needs are denied by maintaining a tough hyper-masculine facade. What remains consistent across genders is that histrionics present a **caricature** of sex roles. Whether seen in the helpless fainting of females, or the hypermasculine conquests of Don Juan males, sex roles are exaggerated to the point of travesty. This results in a fragile, staged kind of adjustment which dissolves under pressure.

Macho men, for example, easily become "little boys" when illness or other trauma cracks the shell of bravado. Industrial accidents with resultant chronic disability are common among male histrionics. Their overreaction to pain, injury, or illness is obvious to family members, yet difficult to escape. Such men exploit others through dependency. A typical histrionic role reversal is that of "disabled" Dad staying home and watching television, while Mom shoulders the responsibilities for keeping the family system running.

In summary, although we tend to notice the exhibitionistic, seductive behaviors of a "Monique," the histrionic style is primarily characterized by (1) impressionistic thinking, (2) overreactive and unstable emotions, and (3) social behaviors which are attention-seeking. Such people are often seen as self-centered, immature, and dependent on others. Let us look more closely at the underlying psychological structure. *So how do we deal w/ them?*

Psychological Style. We will now examine those psychological dimensions which emerge from spending *days or hours* with such persons. At a deeper level of analysis, we find that the histrionic avoids in-depth thinking. As I've already noted, histrionic "thinking" does not consist of clearly-formed ideas, based on factual data. Rather, histrionics live in a world of **impressions**. This is why they're sometimes described as suggestible. How could it be otherwise? Suggestibility is an opposite of critical thought. The scholarly study of a problem, or a careful analysis of a situation, is simply not possible for someone who lives in a world of impressions.

This is why Moniques are so prone to instantly idealize — they really have no other mental contents from which to draw. Alongside blurry impressions of current realities exist romantically colored recollections of the past and capricious plans for the future.

This knight-on-a-white-horse-will-come view of life colors their expectations for the future as well as their romanticized remembrances of the past. And in all of this, facts or data are conspicuously lacking since they would usually spoil the dream.

Such impressionism, however, isn't always about things romantic. The enthusiastic histrionic judgment "He's wonderful!" has its negative counterpart in "He's yucky!" and the switch between emotional states occurs glibly and rapidly, uncomplicated by attention to details or facts. Consequently, the impressionistic world of the hysteric is populated by villains as well as heroes.

When, for example, I asked a histrionic patient why she had married a man whom she knew to be an alcoholic and a drifter, after only two evenings of dating, she replied, "He just had so much pizzazz! It was almost like he put a 'hex' on me!" When I persisted in trying to get more details, she could only respond, "It was his pizzazz that hooked me!" My attempts to elicit further elaboration only brought puzzlement. She couldn't seem to understand the kind of data-based information I was seeking.

Histrionic moods and emotions are fluid, changing rapidly. This is why histrionic persons seem constantly "flooded" with feeling. With an impressionistic mental life and no real cognitions to anchor their experience, these people are always surfing an emotional wave.

Many persons manifest "streaks" of histrionic style in ways quite different from what we've just discussed. There are individuals who delight therapists, faith healers, and hypnotists with quick "cures." They are quick to volunteer for stage demonstrations or other exhibitionistic opportunities. Histrionics are the ones who respond most quickly to altar calls at evangelistic meetings, are "healed" at faith assemblies, or have the "devil cast out" by exorcists in deliverance meetings. Meanwhile other believers — equally devout, but more obsessive-compulsive — sit quietly and observe such happenings.

The histrionic style can be seen in the snake-handling religious cults of the South, the glossolalia of Pentecostal believers, and even in the high levels of emotionalism generated within satanic cults. Wherever an emotionally-laden experience is to be found, a hysteric will be nearby. What is common to all is a frenzy of emotionalism, unaccompanied by reflective cognition.

Histrionic motives typically include a need to be the center of attention. As we've seen, this often includes, on the part of females, coquettish sexual flirtations. The hysteric's self-centeredness frequently includes dramatic displays of helplessness, detailed accounts of victimization, or socially-unaware insistence that her wishes be met. Male histrionics often take pride in their "conquests" and being known as "heartbreakers" or "ladies' men."

Life Style. Looking at the kinds of recurring themes that you notice after you've spent several *months or years* with a histrionic person, there are few surprises. It's simply a matter of observing how the impressionistic thinking, intense emotions, and self-centered social ploys ultimately play out. Major themes in histrionic lives include victim-aggressor, rescue-rape, or child-parent motifs. Often this is carried out with overdone flamboyance, leaving you wondering, "Is she (he) for real?" And you're never quite sure. The caricature-like roles these people assume for themselves and project onto others seem contrived to most of us but are consistent with the histrionic's blurred, impressionistic "reality."

Histrionic Forgiveness

Each personality style results in characteristic ways of giving and receiving forgiveness. Each believer forgives distinctively, and histrionics forgive with flair and flamboyance. *Frothy forgiveness* is what you might expect from histrionics because you know by now they are emotional surfers. It doesn't surprise you that their forgiveness comes, like your A & W root beer, with a frothy head of emotional foam. Like that too-rapidly-poured root beer it's sometimes mostly foam with little substance.

Depending *primarily* on how the histrionic believer *feels at the moment,* forgiveness might be rapid and emotional (with weeping and embracing), or it could be fiercely withheld, or served up with a seething how-dare-you-think-I-would? attitude. Dealing with histrionics is always emotionally "iffy." Forgiveness feels "dicey."

How true! You are not sure you are really forgiven.

51

In this chapter you've met Monique and have become acquainted with the histrionic style. In the following chapter Megan and Daniel will illustrate the psychologically opposite but commonly encountered obsessive-compulsive style.

Chapter 4

How *Personality Styles* Influence Forgiveness

(Obsessive-Compulsive Style)

Megan And Daniel

Megan's aunt was frantic as she poured out her problem: "She's *too* perfect, pastor. I worry that she prays *too much*!"

Not the kind of complaint one typically hears from the relatives of adolescents. Pastor Jim's first impulse was to wonder how a teen could be too good, but he was soon to find out as the distraught aunt poured out her tale:

"I caught her staying up very late at night praying. At first I was pleased that she was so 'devoted,' but then I started to worry. I don't think it's normal for a nineteen-year-old to spend two or three hours a night praying. Is it?"

Jim looked puzzled but didn't directly answer her question. "Please go on," he encouraged.

"Well, I talked with her about it. Explained that God knows our hearts, understands our motives, and willingly forgives us, without our having to beg. She seemed to understand and — can you believe this, Pastor? — promised not to pray so much. But then, a few days later, I found out that Megan would pray briefly before climbing into bed in order to fool her grandmother who slept in the adjoining bedroom. However, after Grandmother's snoring indicated she was sleeping soundly, Megan would crawl back out of bed and pray for another two or three hours! I caught her doing this! How do you punish a child for praying?"

Jim remembered a similar parishioner with a compulsion he'd counseled several years before. Twenty-two-year-old Daniel had come for pastoral counsel regarding his feeling of always being "dirty." It seems that even though he washed his hands upwards of forty or fifty times a day — sometimes using Top Job or Mr. Clean — he couldn't feel they were clean enough. He recounted how his parents had moved to a new neighborhood when he was four years old. Dan distinctly recalled pulling a stool up to the kitchen sink and washing his hands with warm soapy water several times each day, remembering it felt relaxing and warm — "like a mini-jacuzzi for my hands."

The hand washing abated after the first couple years in the new home. During late adolescence, however, whenever Dan felt pressured by school or work, or (as he reluctantly disclosed) after he masturbated, he would wash his hands for twenty or thirty minutes at a time. By age 22 the compulsion had worsened to where he felt totally out of control with it. Jim referred Dan to me for treatment because he felt hand-washing compulsions were out of his league.

After several months of weekly psychotherapy with me, Dan began to understand the sources of his anxiety and his compulsions lessened. He was able to quit trying to become *perfectly* clean, *perfectly* wise, *perfectly* virtuous, *perfectly* punctual, *perfectly* ... you get the idea! Beneath all his strivings was an incipient sense of humor, and he smiled when I once suggested that perhaps he might quit trying to be a composite of Douglas MacArthur, Daniel Webster, John McEnroe, Henry Kissinger, and God!

But Megan's compulsion seemed different. Somehow a "compulsion" to pray didn't seem so bad. Hers seemed like a genuine spiritual problem — about repentance, forgiveness, and the acceptance of God's grace. So Jim took up where her aunt had left off, trying to reason, reassure, and convince Megan that she **was** forgiven. However, after Megan seemingly agreed that she had been forgiven, a more subtle concern gripped her mind. It was one thing to know you were forgiven, but how could you be certain you were "perfect enough"? How could you be sure you'd tried hard enough?

After numerous counseling sessions, prayers, and much reassurance Megan was still plagued with worries about falling short of perfection. Still, she seemed somewhat improved, and after her aunt moved to a nearby town, Pastor Jim didn't hear from them for several years. Recently things seemed to have taken a turn for the worse — or at least Megan's aunt thought so, and she had called her former pastor to seek a referral.

Megan sits in a far corner of my waiting room conspicuously engrossed in *Better Homes and Gardens*. She seems hardly to notice me when I first invite her into my office. Most people leave the magazine they're reading in the waiting room, but not Megan! In fact it becomes, as therapy continues, a kind of "anxiety thermometer" indicating to me how trusting Megan is feeling on a particular day. Megan carries a "security blanket" in the form of a magazine. She hardly looks at me for most of the first session, responding only to direct questions, and then a bit irritatedly as if I were interrupting her important reading.

Early in my career as a psychotherapist, I would have been offended at playing second fiddle to *Better Homes and Gardens*, but by now I know better than to be affronted.

"What brings you here, Megan? How can I be of help?" I begin gently.

"I don't know! You're the doctor!" She snaps from behind the flower-splashed magazine cover.

Now I better understand the experience of people who complain that they have breakfast each morning with the *Wall Street Journal*. Her response is not only abrupt, it's anonymous. How do I converse with a magazine cover? Also, "You're the doctor!" is not a show of respect or admiration; I'm being set up. "You're the genius!" she's sarcastically implying. "You tell me, if you're so intelligent!"

"I'll try to help, but I need some idea of what brought you here," I try again.

"What brought me here is my work supervisor said she thought I could use some counseling because I'm not getting my work finished on time. Of course, what that doesn't tell you is that those deadlines are *her* deadlines; she's on a different schedule than I am. But at least when I do finish a job, it's done right!"

"But," I carefully persist, "didn't Pastor Jim suggest you come see me?"

"Yes, he did." ... (long silence) "So?"

"Well, I just wondered how come he thought it might be good for us to talk."

"How should I know? You can call him on the phone and ask *him*. It's OK with me."

(Cautiously) "But I'd rather hear from you why you went to see your pastor."

"Oh, well! If you've got to know ... I felt guilty because my boyfriend Dan and I got carried away once and nearly had sex together. I prayed about it, but just couldn't feel forgiven. We're planning to get married ... well, that's another thing. Each time he wants to set a date, I feel like I want to break it off, but then we always somehow get back together ... I don't feel good enough for him ... and I don't feel he's good enough for me either! I don't know."

"Hmm," I think, "she's having some difficulty at work, feels guilty about sex, worried about commitment ... that's about it ... she doesn't seem inclined to tell me more."

And so our first psychotherapy session shuffles haltingly along with long periods of silence, interrupted by the polished whisper of glossy pages turning as $800,000-homes, gardens, and prize-winning recipes strut their stuff in front of Megan's intensely focused eyes. She responds to my occasional questions with answers that are brief and precise, neatly clipped, like the green hedges she spends her time scrutinizing. At the close of our session I'm tempted to quip, "I'm sorry I had to interrupt your reading with my questions," but of course I don't.

The next session isn't much better. Once I fail to understand one of her rapid-fire replies and ask, "Could you say that again?" She announces, "I only chew my cabbage once!" Gradually, as time passes, she softens and I begin to uncover the pain she carries inside. Slowly at first, she begins to trust me, warily letting me into her world a few centimeters at a time. Now she even leaves *Better Homes and Gardens* in the waiting room about half the time.

Eventually she shares an incident which took place when she was about six years old, and I understand why she tries so hard to maintain control over her life now.

"We were in the kitchen. My oldest sister was fixing pancakes. We were just eating ... laughing ... having a good time. Mom came downstairs and — thinking about it now — she seemed upset. Looked like she'd been crying. Then — all of a sudden — we all heard a shot! Mom started screaming and ran back upstairs. I still

56

remember seeing the blood. Dad had shot himself. God, it was so awful. We went to stay with my aunt for a year. After that Mom was never the same. Now I think she must have blamed herself, but at the time, I felt like *I* had done something wrong! Like maybe if we hadn't been making pancakes and laughing in the kitchen the whole thing wouldn't have happened. *Now* I know that's stupid, but that's how I felt then."

As her tragic tale unfolds, Megan begins weeping, softly at first, just a few sniffles, but as she recounts the details, her sobbing becomes increasingly intense until her entire body shudders with the memories of that awful Sunday morning.

After this, she no longer brings magazines into the sessions. Her answers are less "rat-a-tat-tat" and she shares her feelings without much prodding on my part.

She and Dan are experiencing little joy and a lot of frustration. Dan blames her, saying she's "too distant." She counterattacks with, "You're only interested in my body ... you never talk to me." Both charges are true but shallow. Not talking is her way of wanting him to reach out for her without having to ask — a safe way to feel cared for, but hardly the recipe for a good relationship. Over the next several months, Megan gradually "thaws." Having disclosed her family secret, she feels the worst is out and she now can talk about why she finds it so difficult to say "I love you" to Dan.

Not surprisingly, when you've been abandoned by your parents (one through suicide, the other through depression) it leaves deep scars. You subconsciously vow you'll never be vulnerable again. One way of doing that is to stay distant. The scariest words in the world become "I love you." Or, even more scary, "I need you."

Dan is a nice enough guy and he really does love Megan, but it baffles him that even while she claims to deeply care about him, and demands that he demonstrate his devotion to her, she remains emotionally aloof.

"She's so careful about everything," he reports, "it's like being engaged to a porcelain doll."

Fortunately, they never sink into name-calling or other destructive tactics. Dan never calls her a "cold fish" or "ice queen." This allows me to help them find each other. Though I spend most of the therapy hours with Megan, Dan occasionally joins us. Megan becomes quite comfortable telling me of her daily stresses, anxieties, and joys. And, as often happens, she also begins sharing her inner life with Dan. Their relationship improves profoundly and they begin enjoying one another more than ever before.

One day, however, I sense something is very wrong because Megan sits in a far corner of the waiting room appearing intensely interested in *Better Homes and Gardens*.

"You seem upset today," I remark. "Well, I am! How did you know? ... Dan's been promoted. His company wants him to move to New York City ... We're moving up the wedding a month, and I guess I'll be moving with him."

Surprises always upset obsessive-compulsive persons, and the anticipated move deeply troubles her. She's lost a little ground and feels the need for familiar defenses against anxiety. This time, however, her hide-behind-the-magazine protection is short-lived, and she puts down her *Better Homes* within the first five minutes of our session, looks directly at me, and begins talking about how much she hates changes.

I review her progress, reminding her how well she and Dan have been getting along. We both know that she's made considerable advances in therapy, slowly growing to trust me, and using the sessions to experiment with being more open about expressing her feelings. She savors my soothing, begins to speak more calmly about the upcoming move.

As we near the end of treatment, I know I'll miss Megan. She hasn't entirely learned to trust me, nor does she fully fathom how profoundly her father's suicide affected her; nonetheless, she has made excellent progress and has promised to seek further therapy with someone in New York City if she begins feeling worse.

At our last session Megan brought me two of her favorite recipes as a parting gift, asking me to promise that I would "at least try them once." As the hour drew to a close, she began quietly sobbing, saying she appreciated my patience with her and that she'd really miss "these sessions" (she couldn't quite say that she'd miss *me*).

Megan illustrates how an obsessive tries to cope with stressful emotions by sitting on them. After her father died and her mother became depressed, Megan learned to muffle her feelings — even good ones. Consequently, as an adult Megan appeared aloof and uptight, but behind her well-fortified defenses was a warm and caring person, a frightened but compassionate lady.

It's been twenty-some years since our sessions, but sometimes while I'm standing in the checkout lane and the clerk is tallying my groceries, I'll notice a *Better Homes and Gardens* among the magazines, and I think of Megan.

Now let's look at some of the general characteristics of obsessive-compulsive persons. **The quest for perfection** permeates all aspects of the obsessive-compulsive's life. Even deciding which item to order on a menu can become a crisis. He wants to try the lasagna *and* the fettuccine but knows he can't order both. Here the issue is not so much avoiding errors as it is making the *perfect* choice. After changing orders several times, only embarrassment prevents him calling the waiter yet another time to get more information about another menu item.

If ordering lunch is such an ordeal, you might imagine what it's like for the obsessive to purchase an automobile or choose a spouse. Salzman (1985) tells of a severely obsessive young man who studied the specifications of all the new cars in order to make the best purchase possible:

> *This process was so involved and became so prolonged that by the time the survey was finished the new models arrived and he had to begin his survey all over again.*
> (1985, p. 67)

Trying to halt this mental see-saw, obsessives often resort to rituals, rules, formulas, or procrastination in order to avoid the risk inherent in deciding. They might use a "color wheel" in combination with a weekly clothes schedule in order to decide which necktie to wear. Typically, if one procrastinates long enough, circumstantial necessities will pre-empt decisions, as when failure to act before a deadline automatically forecloses an alternative while allowing the "forgetful" person to disclaim responsibility for it. Such was the case with Salzman's patient:

59

*This sequence continued for a few years until need fi-
nally forced him to make a choice. He then purchased the
first car he saw on a used-car lot, a car which lacked all
the engineering qualities he had, until then, considered
absolutely essential. He took no responsibility for this
choice, claiming that he was forced into the decision by
the automobile industry and the therapy.* (1985, p. 67)

Completing crucial projects is sometimes extremely difficult
for obsessives who place such a premium on perfection, and for
whom all details must be in order. I've known several obsessive
graduate students whose attempts to write the "perfect" disserta-
tion took the better part of two decades to complete. Some simply
gave up, not because they weren't intelligent enough to complete
the task, but because, like the patient trying to purchase the perfect
automobile, they tried to include *all* the most recent studies. This
attempt — if perfectionistically pursued — is impossible since each
day new data is being published somewhere in the world.

Choosing the "perfect" marriage partner becomes almost impossible for severely obsessive persons. One of my patients had
spent years searching for the right spouse, but each time he'd started
seriously caring about a woman, he would inevitably find a "flaw"
which made further involvement pointless. His dates were either
too beautiful, leading him to feel unattractive by contrast, or not
beautiful enough, leading him to feel he could do better. They were
either too intelligent, leading him to feel inferior, or not intelligent
enough, failing to stimulate him intellectually. And so it had gone,
woman after woman, year after year. It took several months of
intense treatment before he began to see all of this as an elaborate
avoidance, designed to reduce his anxiety about making mistakes.

Avoiding mistake — finding the perfect chicken. We've seen
that obsessives dread decisions, because a choice might not be "perfect," and this in turn erodes their sense of omniscience — the
need to know all and control all. Decisional see-sawing might appear justified in big decisions, involving one's career, marriage
partner, or possibly even the purchase of an automobile. However,
what is distinctive about obsessive-compulsives is the importance
they attach to genuinely trivial decisions.

A colleague told me of a Jewish lady in New York City who spent each Friday searching for the perfect chicken. She wanted to feed her family chicken soup and matzo balls each Friday night and spent the entire day going from one meat market to another, seeking — but never quite finding — the perfect chicken. Such searches, though appearing trivial or inconsequential to others, are of life-or-death importance to obsessives. In many cases, perfectionistic striving becomes "retroactive," permeating not only the present and the future, but contaminating the past as well.

Ogden Nash poetically captures the obsessive-compulsive's difficulties with decisions:

If a Boder Meet a Boder, Need a Boder Cry? Yes.

I haven't much faith in bodings; I think that all bodings are daft bodings.

Forebodings are bad enough, but deliver me from aftbodings.

Aftbodings are what too many of us suffer from subsequent to making decisions even of the most inconsequential and niggling.

Aftbodings prevent people in restaurants from enjoying their haunch of venison, because they keep wondering if they shouldn't have ordered the roast crackling suckling pigling.

Aftbodings are what women are constantly up to their midriffs amid,

Because they are always afraid that the hats or dresses they didn't buy are more becoming than the ones they did.

Aftbodings trouble the young executive who has opted for a martini instead of a bloody mary, and plague the rascally artist who too late feels that he should have forged that Gainsborough instead of this Romney.

Aftbodings are the major cause of insomny.

Consider the lines "Of all sad words ... the saddest are these: 'It might have been!' " whittled by J. G. Whittier;

As an example of aftboding, what could be prettier?

Indeed, I deem this an example of aftboding in excelsis,
Because J. G. Whittier wasn't even boding after his own
decision but somebody else's.
I myself am more and more inclined to agree with Omar
and with Satchel Paige as I grow older:
Don't try to rewrite what the moving finger has writ, and
don't ever look over your shoulder.
(from *There's Always Another Windmill* © 1967. Used
by permission)

Reducing anxiety by being perfect. The master motive behind most obsessive-compulsive behavior is to keep anxiety at manageable levels by controlling everything at all times. The core elements are more psychological than spiritual, and though such persons verbalize concerns about perfection, it is anxiety that drives them. Obsessive-compulsive rituals are some of the most widely used ways of coping with worry. Such patterns spring from our inherent vulnerability. Born into the world totally defenseless, entirely dependent upon others for survival, the human infant's first task is to overcome this primal state of powerlessness. When early traumas are too severe, too chronic, or parental nurturance and soothing is inadequate, this normal striving for control may become a lifelong quest.

The obsessive-compulsive tries through various rituals and maneuvers to deny any helplessness or any dependency on others. In what turns out to be a caricature of competence, he grandiosely attempts to be omnipotent, omniscient, and in need of no one. But maintaining the illusion of invincibility isn't easy and often occurs at the expense of the "softer" emotions.

Emotions are risky. They arise from somewhere deep within the autonomic nervous system and are the least "controllable" of our behaviors. This is why obsessive-compulsives place such a high premium on thinking, on "using your head instead of following your gut." Obsessive-compulsives reduce anxiety by escaping *from* emotion, while histrionics distract themselves from anxiety by escaping *into* emotion.

Social impressions. Obsessive-compulsive persons don't make the kind of "splash" typical of histrionics. The grand entrances and the life-of-the-party effervescence so typical of histrionics are almost totally missing in obsessive-compulsives, who appear overly serious, even boring. Some of the more severe obsessives tend to be regarded by others as "nerds" or "geeks," often bright, but socially out of synch. In less extreme forms they often are the "workaholics," investing extraordinary amounts of time and effort in doing a perfect job. Work achievement tends to be highly valued, while social or recreational pursuits shrivel.

But obsessive-compulsives are not always socially inept, nor do they necessarily lack interpersonal skills; they are often too preoccupied with "important" matters to "waste time" socializing. These are the people who work fourteen-hour days, never take time to vacation; and if once in ten years the rest of the family persuades the obsessive-compulsive to go on a vacation, they usually regret it, because when an obsessive-compulsive person takes a "vacation" it becomes pressure cooked for everyone:

"OK, the first day if we drive for eleven hours and take no more than five minutes for bathroom stops and thirty minutes for lunch and supper stops — we can eat breakfast in the car — we ought to be able to make it to Mount Rushmore by late Monday evening. Then we can be at the monument by the time it opens in the morning, shoot a couple rolls of film and be on the road by 10:30. If we drive most of the day we can make it to ..."

If you've ever vacationed with an obsessive-compulsive parent or spouse, you probably arrived home exhausted, having covered 6,000 miles in ten days, while shooting fourteen rolls of film, all for under four hundred dollars by eating in the car and camping along the way.

The obsessive-compulsive tries always to maintain productivity. Enjoyment *per se* is not a worthwhile use of time and thus never sought directly. In contrast to histrionics, for whom **feelings** are a major focus, obsessives only trust **thoughts** and **productivity**, holding feelings as "soft" and unreliable.

Arriving with an agenda. In therapy the need to be in control manifests itself from the earliest moments. Instead of trusting themselves simply to talk about what's troubling them, they often come to sessions with a prepared list of items to be covered. I've even been provided with xeroxed copies — so that we were both "on the same track." Such organization usually turns out to be an effort to stay on top, i.e., to remain in control.

The following conversation with Jeff, at the beginning of his first session, is illustrative:

Jeff: "Well, what do you want me to talk about?"

Me: "Whatever is troubling you."

Jeff: "Do you want to know about my childhood, or my parents, or what?"

Me: "Whatever seems important to you will be fine."

Jeff: "Why don't you ask me questions? I'll answer your questions. Ask me anything you want to, I'll tell you about it."

Even while appearing to cooperate, Jeff was too guarded to be spontaneous and ultimately waited me out, refusing to talk unless I asked him questions. He responded to open-ended questions with cautious concreteness:

Me: "Well, suppose you tell me what it was like when you were growing up?"

Jeff: "What do you want to know?"

Me: "Tell me about your family."

Jeff: "I had one older sister and two younger brothers. My dad was a carpenter and my mom stayed at home."

Me: "What was the psychological 'climate' like — how everyone got along?

Jeff: "My dad worked a lot. Us kids all did OK in school. My mom kept real busy."

Jeff wasn't specifically trying to be uncooperative, he simply wasn't accustomed to thinking in terms of emotions or feelings, and in a new situation he wasn't about to take any risks.

Managing minutiae. Obsessive-compulsive persons are experts in the management of minutiae. Attention to details, repetition, focusing narrowly on certain facts — these all *seem* to supply soothing predictability amidst life's uncertainties. Thus, if you count cracks in the sidewalk or telephone poles, you can be *certain* that crack number 16 always occurs between cracks 15 and 17, never before 10, and always before 20. You can increase your certainty by knowing that although 16 could be halved to produce two eights, each of which could be further halved to pairs of fours, such symmetry could not be achieved with crack 17. So you learn that certain numbers are "better" than others, and you develop favorites, much as you did among your toys as a child. Numbers become "friends," if I may be allowed a pun, "you can count on."

The alphabet is also "user-friendly," because you can forever depend on those 26 characters to remain predictable. It's a community where it pays to "know your P's and Q's," because they are predictable. Unlike the neighborhood in which you now live, where you can never be certain who might move in next door, P and Q will always be neighbors across town from A and B. Although you can't control who comes and goes next door, you can be assured that P and Q will seldom be seen without U.

Repetition is reassuring. We've seen that while Monique and other histrionics cope with anxiety by blurring, bypassing, or denying facts, Megan, Dan, and other obsessive-compulsives use repetitive rituals to create the illusion of control. Why are some persons trapped in a life of compelling routine? Why do they organize with such desperation? Probably because they've not experienced sufficient soothing during their earliest encounters with stress. In more optimal development parents console and comfort their infants during times of tension, and this is subsequently taken over or **internalized** by the toddler during the early years of childhood.

Ouchy, Ouchy, Ouchy — Internalizing Soothing

My three-year-old neighbor took a nasty spill on her tricycle. Almost immediately, Mom came streaking out of the house, picked up the screaming child, held her closely, kissed her skinned knees and soothingly repeated, "Ouchy, ouchy, ouchy! Poor baby, I know it hurts! ... Ouchy, ouchy, ouchy! Here, let Mamma kiss it." After a few minutes of such comforting Jennifer was again happily riding her tricycle — skinned knees notwithstanding — and had internalized some new skills for dealing with disasters. Some weeks later, I noticed she had again spilled, but this time, instead of screams of distress, I saw her sit down, cross-legged, kiss her own knee, and quietly murmur, "Ouchy, ouchy, ouchy!" Then, without further ceremony, she got back on her tricycle and began to ride.

65

Dan's mother, on the other hand, had been severely depressed during the first four years of his life, and had been emotionally unavailable to soothe and comfort him during critical incidents of stress. Moving to a new neighborhood was just one of the many times he had to manage as best he could on his own. Since he had not experienced — and thus not internalized — parental soothing, he had few internal resources for dealing with danger — even as an adult. He lacked the inner ability to calm himself, so when confronted with stress, he relied on external rituals such as repeatedly washing his hands.

The compulsion to keep, also known as hoarding, is yet another manifestation of the obsessive-compulsive's fear of making a mistake. Hoarding differs from accumulating collectibles for their sentimental value, emotional significance, or financial value. Philatelists collect stamps, phillumenists collect matchbooks, and numismatists collect coins because they are interested in the objects themselves. Even fetishists are driven to collect women's undergarments by an erotic interest in the object. Hoarding, by contrast, is a compulsion to **keep**, which derives not from an interest in the objects, which are often worthless, but from a fear of throwing away something which *might* someday be of use. "After all, you never know when this might come in handy!"

The elderly Collyer brothers lived in their New York Fifth Avenue home until their deaths in 1947, at which time police had to remove 120 tons of junk, among which were fourteen grand pianos, numerous packages of newspapers, and other assorted contents of little real value. What differentiates genuine hobbyists from hoarders are the gum wrappers, Kleenexes, torn movie stubs, old shampoo bottles, rubber bands, strings, newspapers, mayonnaise jars, broken bicycles, and untunable pianos collected by the latter.

Time management is high on the obsessive-compulsive's agenda. Time, like everything else for the obsessive, represents something that needs to be planned and managed (i.e. controlled). Time is pervasive for all of us, yet it moves relentlessly on, seemingly uninfluenced by human forces. As such, it presents great difficulties for the obsessives, eroding their sense of omnipotence. Obsessives typically ignore or minimize the importance of time.

Consequently their time is often organized poorly, and almost always *underestimated.*

Time has contradictory meanings for obsessives. On the one hand they invariably try to cram too much into a short time, defying the limits that time puts on us all, and typically being late for appointments or deadlines. On the other hand, she expects others to be punctual, efficient, and accurate in their time estimates so that they do not "waste" her time with tardiness, and so forth. Thus the obsessive-compulsive's relationship to time is ambivalent. On the one hand, he keeps close track of it (typically setting his watch to "beep" every hour); on the other hand she tries to deny its importance by not realistically factoring it into her plans.

Limited affectionate responses, often seen in obsessive-compulsives, are more a product of their machinelike qualities, their intellectualized attempts to analyze and control everything, than a genuine lack of caring. Nonetheless, the families of obsessives often feel emotionally neglected or crowded out by work and other activities. In psychotherapy, I've seen defensive, intellectually aloof obsessives become genuinely warm and caring, but only after months, or even years, of treatment.

How Obsessives Forgive

Calculated — "one-for-me-one-for-you" — forgiveness is what you'll likely feel when forgiven by an obsessive-compulsive believer. You'll feel more like you've attended an IRS audit than a church picnic. You'll sense you've been thoroughly examined and be thankful when the ordeal is over. You'll be "rejoicing" all right, but primarily because it's over rather than in the swell of "amazing grace" you've experienced. Also, you'll worry about ever "slipping up" again, because you feel as if you're dealing with a "moral elephant" who never forgets! Oh, yes, they'll dutifully dispense another dose of pardon as required by the seventy-times-seven formula, but it won't be easy, and they'll let you know.

But as we've seen with Megan, there is a genuinely caring core to many obsessives, though it is often well hidden behind a facade of external iciness. They are hardly able to *receive* forgiveness, so it isn't surprising they have such difficulty *dispensing* forgiveness.

67

When you really understand their psychological dynamics — when you know they're not withholding "on purpose" — it becomes easier to tolerate their rigid "unforgiving" approach to life. As you appreciate how important order is in their world, how much they fear risk, how phobic they are of the unexpected, you begin to discern how devastating they find mistakes, both in themselves and in others.

Consequently, a simple "I'm sorry" just doesn't cut it. A glib "Oh, that's OK" hardly suffices. For obsessives genuine forgiveness almost requires a change of personality and that's difficult. So the next time you encounter the "unforgiving" rigidity of an obsessive, I hope you'll be able to dig a little deeper into your own understanding and find it a bit easier to forgive.

In the next chapter, we'll consider a few more styles, but a bit more briefly. I'll try not to be "obsessive." OK? Stay with me.

Chapter 5

How *Personality Styles* Influence Forgiveness

(Shy/Shameful Styles)

You know how it feels! A dreadful, warm, crawling sensation beginning somewhere in the pit of your stomach and creeping slowly up your body, gaining intensity until the back of your neck feels like a hot iron and your face flushes red. **Shame.** It makes you want to contract into a tiny ball of nothing and disappear. It's an awful experience.

Psychologically naked, mortified, you want to hide. Fortunately for you, it's probably happened only a few times in your life. But what if you felt those same sensations — only a little less intensely — each time you met a new person? What if you began to feel your face warm with self-consciousness each time someone asked you a question? What if your neck tingled with embarrassment each time someone spoke to you? That's what life is like for shy/shameful personalities. They may not blush brightly enough for you to see it, but each time they interact with a stranger, enter a new social situation, or just try to make small talk with an acquaintance that awfulness starts creeping up their back.

Most of us feel bashful at times and often become overly concerned with how others evaluate us, but shy/shameful persons are so sensitive to criticism and so devastated by disapproval that social situations become excruciating. They are preoccupied with doing the right thing in order to avoid mortification. Not surprisingly they tend to avoid social situations or occupations which involve much contact with other people. However, they usually *wish* they could be more friendly and outgoing. They *want* friends but are afraid of saying something foolish, worried that others might ridicule them. They dread being embarrassed by blushing, crying, or showing signs of uneasiness in the presence of others.

69

Shy/shameful people usually dislike anything that deviates from their usual routine, because new endeavors, especially in the social arena, carry the risk of being exposed — of appearing foolish or inept. So in their minds they exaggerate the difficulties, risks, or dangers of any new social activity and avoid stepping out. Consequently, they find themselves isolated, with few friends.

Shy/shameful individuals yearn for friendship and acceptance. They long for a partner with whom they can be real, but they presume their chances for finding intimacy are slim. Consequently, dislike of self snowballs, they become less confident, and their skills in social or sexual matters become dwarfed.

As we shall see, this style usually begins in childhood with experiences of intense shame. Shyness is the **outward** timid behavior we see, shame the **inward** awfulness they feel. Cassandra is a case in point.

Cassandra

Six-year-old Cassandra's brown eyes flashed with anger as she slammed her backpack onto the freshly-waxed kitchen floor. "I ... I ... I'm *never* going back!" she wailed. "I *hate* school!" With that, her anguished emotions abruptly shifted, anger giving way to grief, tears tumbling down her freckled cheeks while great sobs shook her little frame. These after-school outbursts, accompanied as they inevitably were by resolutions never to attend again, were becoming alarmingly regular. And if the pain to Cass seemed unbearable, Mom found it excruciating because she understood the lifelong implications.

By some cruel fate Cassandra had suffered a blood clot that blocked her cerebral artery, leaving her in a coma for three days. Although she'd recovered, after a fashion, there had been irreversible brain damage. It was "very rare," doctors had told her parents, for five-year-olds to suffer strokes, but this brought them little comfort, and the long hospitalization devastatingly disrupted Cass' life.

Prior to the stroke, she had excelled in school, easily surpassing her peers. After six weeks in kindergarten, she'd been placed in the gifted track and was soon reading and doing arithmetic normally reserved for children in the third and fourth grades. Now, as she limped off the bus to her waiting mom, it was some of the very same children she'd academically "blown away" who jeered, "See ya tomorrow, brace leg!"

How little Cass hated those words! "Brace leg," "fake leg," "wood leg," "peg leg," "retard" — those cruel nicknames found their way to the farthest alcoves of her psyche. Although she laughed along with her playmates and tried to pretend it didn't bother her, she suffered agonizing humiliation each time another child commented about her brace. Her shame was searingly intense with each awkward step in the hallway between classes or on her way to lunch.

The stroke had left her with significant loss of motor function on the right side. Her right eyelid drooped slightly, her shoulder sagged, her right hand was clenched in a permanent fist, and she required a brace on her right leg in order to walk. While still in the hospital she'd overheard the doctors tell her parents she would always suffer from a "claw hand" and "claw toes" on the right side of her body. "Oh, Mommy!" she'd screamed. "Am I going to grow claws?" How do you explain to a five-year-old that "claw" toes means spasticity of the metatarsal phalangeal joints?

Her first day back at school had been nightmarish. While she'd awkwardly maneuvered her cumbersome prosthesis down the hall, her peers had gawked with unabashed curiosity.

"Look! Cassy's got a wood leg!"

"T'aint neither wood, it's plastic!"

A kindly teacher had disrupted the "show" by ordering the other children outside to play. But as the group had laughingly exited, Cassy heard the sing-song, "Cassy's got a brace leg. Cassy's got a brace leg."

Ten years have passed since that first dreadful day back at school, but it could easily have been ten minutes. The memories remain lucid — revived with each step she takes. Now the carefully camouflaged limp of adolescence replaces the awkward shuffle of the six-year-old. She lifts, twists, swings, and drops her right leg with the grace of a ballerina. Yet deep inside she still feels naked, exposed, knowing that others notice even though they no longer ask those awful "What-happened?" questions. Though her right foot drops quietly, with an almost imperceptible twist, to Cassandra each step sounds like an air hammer in a cathedral. The shameful thump, thump, thump she "hears" whenever she walks nearly bursts the inside of her head. Like most people who are noticeably "different," Cass lives suspended between outward "niceness" and inner rage.

Nearly every moment of every day Cass struggles to work out an existence that allows her some expression of rage without completely cutting off her social life. Not an easy balancing act.

When she was younger, she often indulged in revengeful fantasies against children who ridiculed her. She dreamed of hurting them in slow, torturous ways. Her favorite fairy tale was "Hansel and Gretel" — with slight modifications. When she came to the part where Gretel pushed the wicked witch into the oven and slammed the door, she imagined it was one of her "friends" who'd recently been teasing her who was locked in the oven, slowly cooking to a crisp. She savored stories like "The Ugly Duckling" and "The Frog Prince" where homely creatures turned into swans and princes. Now these favorite fairy tales have been replaced with fantasies of miracle cures, natural prostheses, and the winning of beauty contests.

Good-Me, Bad-Me

There are really two Cassandras. The private Cass is deeply humiliated, shameful, and angry. The public Cass is smiling, compliant, and seen by others as "that sweet young girl with the problem." She is split right down the middle, psychologically as well as neurologically. She experiences her left side — the side on which her motor functions remain intact — as her "good" side. Her right side houses the "crippled" Cass and is experienced as "bad."

Cassandra's case illustrates how the powerful emotions of shame and anger, when chronically present early in childhood, fracture the personality. A deep split develops between the public "nice" me and the private enraged me. This divided self is difficult to mend. The "nice" and angry selves do not naturally come together; instead they drift further apart, widening the gap.

Like the obese person who feels compelled to be "jolly," the repeatedly ridiculed person is publicly pleasant, feeling there is no other choice. But the chronic teasing and taunting drives their private life into ever deepening hostility. Most persons with "shameful" handicaps seesaw between rage and "niceness." Like Cass, children with tics, seizure disorders, speech problems, club feet, or other publicly-ridiculed features are usually "nice" and angry. The split may not be as dramatic as the left-right vertical split that accompanies Cassandra's neurological problems, but it is nonetheless real. Stutterers experience a "good" (fluent) me and a "bad" (stuttering) me because children will always tease stutterers — guaranteed! And it usually begins when the child enters school for the first time.

Leaving home is a difficult transition for most children, but the "different" child is particularly vulnerable to ridicule. Tension no longer occurs in rhythms of eating, elimination, and diapering; what matters now is how many friends you have, if you read easily, and whether Teacher likes you. The crucial concerns are social, not physical, and newly-formed relationships remain fragile. Mocking laughter is nowhere more prominent and painful than among the child's own peer group, and it is ridicule by "friends" which is most devastating for the young child. Even though a teacher may provide some protection, this is often at the cost of becoming "teacher's pet."

In these early school years anything unusual attracts "interest" (ridicule). Six-year-olds have not attained the social grace of not staring when someone with a handicap is present. Quite the contrary, it arouses their unabashed interest. This is the age at which children ask, "Mommy, why does that man have red spots on his head?" or "Daddy, why is that lady so fat?" or "How come that man doesn't have hair on his head?"

Thus, the stutterer is doomed to hearing: "Hey T...T...Tony! I'll bet you can't s...s...s...say P...P...Peter P...P...Piper picked a pack of pickled p...p...peppers."

One of the enigmas of children is the glibness with which they engage in verbal cruelty. Possibly, like adult gossip, it serves to reduce personal anxiety about self by focussing on others. Like heat-seeking missiles, children sense vulnerabilities in one another and attack at that point. The obese child is called "fatso," while the flat-chested adolescent girl is called "ironing board." The intellectually slow child is disparagingly labelled "retard," while the child with thick glasses becomes known as "four eyes" or "coke bottles." Few children escape unscathed because almost everyone has "defects" — none of us is perfect.

Ridicule Leads to Shame. Shame is not ridicule; it is the *result* of ridicule. Teasing and derision continue to reverberate as "self-talk" long after the actual incidents of torment have passed. Thus, although shame originates as an interpersonal social experience, it quickly becomes **internalized** and is then experienced as part of the self. Then it no longer suffices to fantasize about destroying the oppressors out there, because the enemy is within.

Shame is extraordinarily powerful in its ability to shrivel self-esteem. "I could have crawled into a hole and died!" is how this experience is typically described. Shame overpowers with suddenness. Experienced as a surge of awfulness that quickly rises from the abdomen to heat the back of the neck and further humiliate the self by blushing the face, there seems to be no escape and no way to hide one's humiliation from the observing eyes of others. This kind of inescapable intensity accounts for the tenacity with which shame and self become fused as the **shameful self**. Ridicule cannot easily be shaken off or displaced. It seeps inward, engulfing and permeating the developing sense of self.

Anger Defends the Self. Ridicule pushes experience inward — engulfing the self with shame, anger serves to protect the self by fighting back. The angry self seeks to destroy the tormenter and thus end the humiliation. Even when anger is suppressed and goes "underground" as bitterness, resentment, or hostility its goal is to remove the teaser. The inner life of resentful persons is rich with revenge. Like Cassandra, most teased persons have vivid fantasies of harming and hurting their tormenters. Anger allows the shamed or humiliated self to "fight back." Instead of withdrawing into nothingness, it allows one to act powerfully — at least in fantasy — against one's persecutors.

We've seen that shame and anger pull in opposite directions — shame shriveling the self, anger exploding it. Thus, in normal

74

circumstances anger serves a defensive function, enabling the child to fight back. However, when an actual handicap is present the child often has internal conversations like the following:

> *They're right. I deserve to be laughed at because I do stutter, [or have a "claw hand," or have seizures, etc.] I don't have a right to be angry. If I get mad, they'll just tease me more. The best thing is to laugh along with them.*

Unfortunately, although such an approach buys the child a bit of temporary peace, it tends to perpetuate the cycle. Such children often act in excessively "nice" ways and take their handicaps "in stride." Actively holding back their destructive rage, they inadvertently encourage more of the same. Other children noticing that the teasing is tolerated — even "enjoyed" by the other person, since they are laughing too — continue their destructive ridicule. As such vicious cycles continue, the rage intensifies, making it even more impossible to express. Living this way can be infuriating, but since even mild irritation is not expressed by the target child, such fury never finds public expression, and the chasm between anger and niceness deepens. Such children "forgive" far too easily and fool even themselves into thinking that teasing doesn't bother them. They feel compelled to act nice but are deeply angry inside.

Try to imagine the psychological experience of the handicapped. Is it any wonder that they are nearly always "nice"? If once a month you experienced a grand mal seizure and regained consciousness to find yourself lying flat on the ground — possibly in your own urine or feces — with a circle of frightened faces looking down at you, think of how terribly embarrassed you would feel. Think of how hard you would try to be "nice" the other 29 days of the month to "make up" for such a "shameful" episode. And when the pale faces and frightened eyes belong to other third graders in your room — people you have to see each day — the humiliation can be almost unbearable.

Much of Cassandra's therapy involved helping her to get in touch with her seething rage and helping her accept it as okay. She began to share her fantasies of what she wanted to do to those who had teased and humiliated her throughout her lifetime. Once the repression dam burst, the rage came pouring out, accompanied by violent sobbing and vivid descriptions of painful revenge visited on her persecutors. This "nice" young girl, who apparently dealt so admirably with her problems, would have rivaled a Gestapo torture expert in her malevolent machinations.

However, once she began to recognize and talk about her anger she began to heal. The gap between her niceness and her rage began to narrow. She learned that expressing anger didn't negate her goodness, that most people live with both pleasure and frustration. She became more comfortable with the co-existence of negative and positive emotions and allowed herself to express annoyance, irritation, and other anger-related feelings more easily. She didn't instantly "forgive" whomever had teased her or laugh along with others at herself. This caused some initial problems with her family and friends, who had considered Cass someone whom "you could count on" always to be cheerful, and so forth. But she gradually traded in her attempts to be like Mother Teresa for a much less perfectionistic view of herself. This allowed her not only to express her anger, but also to reduce the internal shame arising from her private world of rage.

String

"String Bean" is what he'd been called for most of his childhood and adolescence, but as he grew to adulthood it was shortened to simply "String." Though awkward in most sports, he was a natural for basketball. When parked under the hoop, blocking shots and grabbing rebounds, being tall seemed briefly OK. Otherwise his spindly frame was a constant source of embarrassment to him.

It was in the second grade, on Saint Patrick's Day, when he wore a green shirt with matching green trousers that he was "discovered." "Hey look!" one of the other students excitedly exulted, "Billy looks like a string bean!" The children had burst into laughter, Billy had responded by blushing crimson, and that was it. His destiny was sealed. In that single searing moment his future was fixed. From then on, he would be known as "String Bean," "Jolly Green Giant," "Beanstalk," or "String." Prior to that he'd been called "Skinny" or "Boney Mahoney," but now the "green" names stuck — painfully, shamefully. Even now, in his mid-forties, whenever an acquaintance from high school days ran into him, it was "How ya doing, String? Long time no see!" He doubted any of them knew his name was actually William. He would gladly have traded Willie, Bill, or even William for one of his "green" names.

As he sat in my office, obese and depressed, it was difficult to imagine this 350-pound man as a scrawny, skyscraping adolescent. He was extremely discouraged because his physician had recently told him he would soon need a knee replacement if he didn't lose at least a hundred pounds. Bad medical news was not new to him. He'd often been warned about risks associated with his chronic high blood pressure and other weight-related problems, but in recent months the pain in his knees had become unbearable and he'd finally gone to a specialist to have it checked out. Arthritis ran in his family, but the physician told him that the pain in his knee joints was being profoundly worsened by his weight. X-rays revealed very little cartilage remaining to cushion the joints and it seemed that a replacement was going to be inevitable. Nonetheless, he'd been told he could put this off by losing weight. Furthermore, once the replacement had been done, it would have to be repeated if he didn't bring his weight down, because artificial joints wear out just like the original ones.

Bill was confident that he could lose the weight, but ironically, it frightened him. Most people remember their "skinny" days with longing. "I wish I weighed what I did when I got married!" is a common lament among dieters. Not so with Bill. He had consciously worked to gain weight in order to put behind him forever the painful memories associated with being a "string bean." Now, faced with the prospect of knee surgery, he was psychologically stymied. He knew he must lose weight, he consciously said he wanted to lose weight; but a deep unconscious part of him was terrified at the prospect of becoming slender, and this paralyzed him.

It was only through intensive psychotherapy, combined with hypnosis, that Bill was able comfortably to imagine himself slender. Once he got past this psychological hurdle, the actual process of losing the weight wasn't as difficult as he'd imagined. Bill lost 94 pounds and still has his original knees.

Shame In Ordinary People
What Makes You Ashamed? Most persons are ashamed of numerous personal characteristics. Shape or size of nose, color of eyes, thickness of eyebrows, distance between front teeth, angle at which ears are attached to the head, size of breasts or penis, presence of acne or birthmarks, these are the items people include on the list of "Things I don't like about myself." Although the list seems to change with maturity, it remains essentially similar; worries about acne are simply replaced by worries about wrinkles, with neither the adolescent nor middle-aged adult enthralled with his or her epidermis. Cosmetics manufacturers translate such shame into profits measured in billions of dollars. Adolescents can't stand the color of their hair; middle-agers abhor the absence of it. Nails are never right, depending on your age, sex, and stress level; they are either dirty, ragged, broken or chewed — but never right.

Ridicule and the resultant shame often target some part of the body evaluated as "different" (e.g., a club foot, large nose, small genitals, and so forth.) This can sabotage one's pride of ownership. "I hate my body!" — a phrase which clinicians often hear from the obese — occurs among the general population as well, often in a more subtle form, targeting specific bodily zones: "I hate my ears ... crooked nose ... chubby hands ... complexion ... eyebrows, and so forth."

Even nonphysical characteristics are singled out for "shame focus" if they're perceived as part of the persona. The thick lenses required for clear vision, the hearing aid that's impossible to conceal completely, the size 46 trousers, the "ugly" shoes one has to wear in order to accommodate arch supports — all such accessories are experienced as liabilities and devalue the person in the eyes of others and self.

Average people are plagued by numerous "imperfections" of which they — more than others — are aware. Most suffer throughout life with a diminished sense of self because so few of these "blemishes" are repairable at reasonable cost. While orthodontia

78

can revamp crooked teeth, and contact lenses can replace "coke bottle" glasses, few people have access to more elaborate interventions such as face lifts, breast implants, "tummy tucks," and the like. Most suffer silently, their misery being continually exacerbated by comparison with more-perfect-than-life caricatures created by Hollywood, *People* magazine, *GQ*, and television.

Ridicule rapidly turns to shame, and is "preserved" by its internal nature, and by the splitting of personality into an angry self and a "nice" self. Although children appear psychologically resilient, they are in fact extremely vulnerable to shame.

Nicknames

Nicknames, like flea collars and eyeglasses, simply become a part of those on whom they're placed. Unlike flea collars and glasses, however, they insidiously destroy their carriers rather than assist them to achieve a better quality of life. And it is their taken-for-granted, accepted-as-part-of-me quality which makes them so dangerous. They are subtle but insidious, not innocuous.

Abuse Often Begins At Home. We've seen how damaging ridicule can be to the developing child's psyche. Tragic as taunting is when it occurs among one's childhood playmates, it is even more deplorable when parents or siblings are the source of such verbal abuse. Family therapists are all too well acquainted with the many cases where a child is called "Shorty," "Bones," "Beefy," "Dumbo," "Meathead," and so forth, by other family members in "fun." ("Fun" is a euphemism for ridicule.) Even in the rare cases where such names are genuinely affectionate "pet" names, they often do not mean the same thing outside the family.

"Bud-Susie." Nicknames are not restricted to physical characteristics, often being based on behavioral reactions of the target child. Johnny, a fourth-grader, gave his classmates the "scoop" on his little brother Patrick who was entering school for the first time: "If you call him 'Bud,' " Johnny informed his friends, "he'll get mad, and if you call him 'Susie,' he'll cry."

Thereafter Johnny's little brother became known throughout the school as "Bud-Susie," a name that stuck for most of his elementary years.

79

"Peabody." A college student told me — with anguish — of his childhood struggles with nocturnal enuresis (night-time bedwetting). The most distressing part of the experience was not the bedwetting, but the fact that somehow the "kids at school" found out and nicknamed him "Peabody." This name, of course, remained long after he had conquered the enuresis, a constant reminder of his previous failures and humiliation.

Reducing Shame At Home And School

Parents and teachers ought to do all they can to eliminate shame-producing ridicule which occurs in the form of teasing, name calling, and other home and school unkindnesses. The following are guidelines:

1. NEVER SPEAK DISPARAGINGLY ABOUT ANYTHING WHICH CANNOT BE *EASILY* CHANGED:

[OK] "That green shirt doesn't go with those blue pants."

[Not OK] "If you keep gaining weight, those slacks are going to split."

[OK] "Eating green apples may cause your stomach to hurt."

[Not OK] "Please talk more slowly, or you'll never get over stuttering."

2. FOCUS ON BEHAVIOR *NOT* PERSONALITY:

[OK] "When I find toys strewn around the house — broken because they were not put away — I get really upset!"

[Not OK] "Why are you so messy?"

[OK] "I'm irritated that grape juice got spilled on the carpet. This wouldn't have happened if the house rule about not eating in front of the television had been followed."

[Not OK] "You spilled your juice again — for the life of me, I can't figure out why you're so clumsy!"

3. DO NOT USE OR ALLOW OTHERS TO USE NEGATIVE NICKNAMES: This is a bit tricky, because attention is usually reinforcing and if you make a "big deal" out of occasional teasing by siblings or playmates, it can backfire and worsen the ridicule. It's almost impossible to police the playground, hallways, or locker rooms — which is where name calling often occurs — but at the very least, the child's home (and homeroom) ought to be a ridicule-free environment.

[OK] "Slowpoke, slowpoke, I bet I can eat my lunch faster than you can!"

[Not OK] "Debbie is a dumbo; Debbie is a dumbo!" "Freddie is a fatso; Freddie is a fatso!" "Dougy is a klutz; Dougy is a klutz!"

The sound of sing-song rhyming should immediately capture the attention of parent or teacher, as vividly as the sound of screeching tires followed by shattering glass. In both instances someone is likely to be hurt — badly.

4. TEACH YOUR CHILDREN NOT TO TEASE: Young children do not realize how damaging words can be. They really believe that "sticks and stones can break my bones, but words will never hurt me." When three-year-old Matthew pulls Fido's ears and bursts out laughing when the dog yelps, he is not so much cruel as uninformed. He doesn't realize he's hurting the dog.

Children need to be taught kindness in words as well as in behaviors. It isn't something they pick up naturally. A couple generations ago, the teaching of "manners" was considered at least as important as the three R's, but today it seems to have dwindled in importance. The wise man said it well: "Pleasant words are a honeycomb, sweet to the soul and healing to the bones" (Proverbs 16:24).

5. TEACHERS, DON'T LET CHILDREN "CHOOSE UP TEAMS" FOR ANY GAMES — BEING CHOSEN LAST IS SOMETHING A CHILD MAY CARRY THE REST OF HER/HIS LIFE: Instead, line children up and count off odd-even teams. Or assign teams on the basis of the alphabet. *Do not* allow them to choose among themselves on the basis of skill, because this will be affirming only for the first couple or three chosen, after which it will become progressively discounting, ending with profound shame for the "last one chosen."

An appropriate goal for parents and teachers would be the total eradication of shame from the lives of all children. Doubtless this will never be achieved, but just as we seek to save our natural environment by reducing pollutants, we ought to strive to reduce drastically "toxins" like shame in the social environment.

How Shameful/Shy People Forgive

Shameful people forgive too quickly. They're ready to say, "It's OK," even before you say you're sorry. That's because their "forgiveness" is based on a sense of personal inferiority. For most of their lives they've been on the damaging, hurtful end of ridicule. They've been scorned, derided, teased, mocked, and shamed, until they deeply believe they're sub-human specimens. Who are they to demand equality? Who are they to deny someone else forgiveness?

Consequently, when encountering such persons, we must not accept their "forgiveness" too readily. It's usually safe to surmise that beneath the external "That's OK," or behind their apparent laughter at themselves, is a smoldering rage or a deep hatred, directed both at themselves and at their tormenters.

Genuine forgiveness in such cases will involve a longer process of counseling, camaraderie, companionship, or friendship that allows them to feel safe enough to "be real." Then, after authentic discussions about anger and resentment — without superficial short-circuiting via phoney "forgiveness" — genuine healing can result.

In this chapter we've considered how the early childhood experiences of being teased or humiliated translate into shame-permeated personalities. We've seen how this is intensified in cases where genuine physical disabilities exist. In the next chapter we will examine shame-permeated personalities which arise not from teasing, physical defects, or other **external** sources, but from **perfectionistic** attitudes within one's mind. And we will come to see that **perfectionism** is the polar opposite of **forgiveness**, the very antithesis of mercy. And sadly, Christians sometimes inadvertently cause shame by setting unachievable goals for themselves and others.

Chapter 6

How *Personality Styles* Influence Forgiveness

(The Perfect Ones)

Case Illustrations

The following case is from the author's (personal memory) files:

I remember when I was a young boy that our family used to attend camp meeting once a year. These were old-fashioned revival meetings with tents, fervent evangelists, and ever-present calls to repentance and revival. Late one Sunday evening, when the preacher's fervor had reached a particularly high pitch, and my guilt for numerous boyhood sins had followed in its wake, I hit the sawdust trail. Finding myself at the front of the tent I was prayed over by the preacher and felt thoroughly cleansed of all my sins.

For a few glorious moments, I felt as pure as I've ever felt in my life, but this is the only time in over fifty years that the disparity between my real self and my ideal self was gone. I was, for a few magnificent moments, *perfect*! But it would be short-lived, and I knew it. A part of me knew that in a short time, my mischievous self would again sabotage my ideal self and I would shamefully fail yet another time. I would be lucky if I remained perfect until the next morning.

My life as a Christian has been a long series of such failures accompanied by shame. And I suspect I'm not alone. Because everyone who has a Xerox of the Incarnate God for an ideal self is also doomed to a life of shame.

Striving to be perfect is not restricted to a particular denomination, but is seen among Protestants, Catholics, and Jews, as is illustrated in the following cases reported by Rapoport (1991):

83

Marion, now 26, used to pray briefly before hopping into bed when she was 12. Her grandmother, who slept in the next room, heard the noise from the bedsprings and assumed her granddaughter had finished praying. After her grandmother began to snore, Marion crept out of bed and prayed for three more hours. (p. 97)

During my residency training in Boston, I was assigned Audrey as a clinic patient. A thin nervous woman of 28, with hair pulled back in a bun, Audrey was preoccupied with prayer and confession. Her daily absences from her two little girls to attend dozens of weekly confessions just added to her guilt. (p. 173)

Sally, a bright, blonde sixth-grader, had looked forward to her Confirmation. Getting a new dress and having her aunt so proud of her outweighed all the hard work. But a few weeks before the big day she started having crying spells, couldn't sleep, and lost ten pounds. It all began suddenly, when Sally was doing a class punishment assignment. She thought she wasn't doing it properly, that she was "sinning." I'm always doing something wrong, she felt. The feeling stayed with her. (p. 171)

In grade school Daniel was seen by family and friends as a bright, thoughtful, friendly child who had grown into a "good kid" and B student. He was popular throughout grade and middle school. For a very brief period while in seventh grade, Daniel had worried about germs and would "blow germs away" when anyone near him sneezed or coughed ...

Tenth grade was when things really got difficult. Daniel changed schools and his grandmother died from cancer a month before school opened. Daniel's fear of germs returned and to "prevent potential illness" he would wash his hands up to thirty times each day. Scrutinizing all silverware, dishes, and glasses for specks of dirt or food, he would even wash all money he received from any source ...

> *As the school year progressed, Daniel decided to "be-*
> *come kosher," though his family only loosely observed*
> *Jewish rituals and practices. He severely limited the va-*
> *rieties of food he was willing to eat, going far beyond the*
> *requirements of keeping kosher.* (p. 177)

Rapoport discusses these cases in some detail, illustrating how obsessive-compulsive disorder manifests itself among the religious. Known clinically as **scrupulosity**, such moral fastidiousness is not a new phenomenon, having apparently been prevalent among the Pharisees, whom Christ characterized as "straining at gnats, while swallowing camels" — a loss of perspective characteristic of the obsessive-compulsive mind.

The remainder of this chapter will deal not with scrupulosity so severe as to be characterized as **disease**, but rather with a more moderate yet widespread **unease** which I shall characterize as the epidemic of shame.

Shame: The Underside Of Christianity

Shame is currently receiving some long overdue attention among serious students of human behavior (e.g., Kaufman, 1985; Morrison, 1989; Nathanson, 1987; Wurmser, 1981). Among popular writers such as Bradshaw (1988) shame has been so expanded as to become the basis for almost every known emotional problem, including shyness, codependency, narcissism, borderline personality, paranoia, criminality, and addictions. Yet puzzlingly, Bradshaw also sees shame as "the source of spirituality." Although some Christian writers (Dobson, 1974) have focused on how to develop healthy self-esteem, or how to avoid damaging the self-esteem of the special-needs children, shame itself has not received much serious attention except in a glib bumper-sticker kind of way. Slogans such as "Smile God Loves You" or "God Doesn't Create Junk" may sound therapeutic but probably do little to repair seriously damaged personalities.

Guilt vs. Shame. It is important to distinguish between guilt and shame. Psychologists generally agree that guilt has an appropriate place in the functioning of the healthy personality. Frequently, however, we find guilt severely out of proportion to wrongdoing, persisting after appropriate confession and amends have been made, or associated with self-dislike or unrelenting remorse. Such guilt is harmful and requires treatment.

Nonetheless, healthy guilt — in appropriate doses — facilitates normal psychological development, and the absence of guilt in the face of wrongdoing is the hallmark of the psychopathic or the antisocial personality.

Shame, on the other hand, is almost always destructive. Morris (1976, p. 62) states: "One cannot be forgiven one's shame and punishment does not divest one of it." Kaufman (1985, p. 8) observes: "To feel shame is to feel *seen* in a painfully diminished sense." He further elaborates that "shame is an impotence-making experience because *it feels as though* there is no way to relieve the matter, no way to restore the balance of things."

Whereas appropriate guilt can encourage confession which may lead to forgiveness, shame leads to concealment out of fear of further damage to the self. While healthy guilt arises as a result of wrongdoing, or sometimes even from planning to carry out wrongful behaviors, shame usually results from childhood ridicule and teasing, or from a failure to live up to the expectations of others. Shame is seldom helpful; it does not lead to healing, growth, or reparations. It tends either to cause depression or to spur perfectionistic efforts to make up for one's deficiencies.

An appropriate goal for Christians would be to maintain healthy guilt about wrongdoing, without becoming swamped with shame about trivial mistakes. Too often, however, shame is generated by well-meaning parents, teachers, and clergy — by the very Christians who seek to heal it. We now turn our attention to how shame is generated.

External And Internal Shame Generators

As we've seen in the previous chapter, shame is frequently generated by ridicule or teasing coming from outside oneself — often from one's "friends" or siblings. Most of us can recall painful childhood experiences of being teased or embarrassed. Such searing moments, in which we were the target of ridicule, are not easily forgotten. Possibly, like adult gossip, teasing serves to reduce personal anxiety about self by focusing on others. Too often children treat differences among themselves with derision and teasing.

Ridicule Produces Internal Shame. As we've shown in the previous chapter, ridicule produces shame. Chronic and intense derision often reverberates as hurtful "self-talk" long after the actual incidents of torment have passed, and in this way shame becomes internalized. Thus, although much shame originates interpersonally — outside oneself — from social experiences, it quickly becomes "owned" as part of the self. (Kaufman, 1985, p. 7) Subsequently it can be generated from within — by self-talk — which keeps it going long after the taunting or mocking has ceased. In this way most shame becomes self-perpetuating, even though it begins with teasing or nicknames.

In addition to teasing or ridicule by peers, there are other external shame generators. In our highly comparative culture, where we constantly measure ourselves against athletes, movie stars, and other "beautiful people" who excel in their pursuits, we are prone to diminish ourselves — feel ashamed — even if no one actively points out our inadequacies.

Once internalized, shame becomes potentially more destructive because it continues to reverberate privately — even when there is no one "out there" to tease, ridicule, or humiliate. Internalized shame is experienced as a seeping sense of badness, permeating the self with toxic tides of self-censure and inferiority.

On the whole, the net effect of Christianity has probably been to reduce externally-triggered shame. Jesus' example of kindness toward the lame and the blind, His concern for the hungry and homeless, and His psychological encouragement of the despised and marginalized of His day have been reflected in the teachings and practice of the church — admirably at times. Following the golden rule of treating others as we ourselves would like to be treated has sensitized many to the wrongness of teasing, ridicule, and other forms of shaming. Yet at the same time, Christians have also caused much shame.

Real Self And Ideal Self. Psychoanalysts speak of the ego and of the ego ideal, which is a part of the superego — the moral arm of personality. For clarity, I will simply refer to the **real** self and the **ideal** self. The ideal self is part of the mental equipment we loosely call "conscience." The ideal self is not so much a moral watchdog — reprimanding us when we err — as it is an internal image of what we might become if we behaved properly at all times. The ideal self includes goals, dreams, and visions of ourselves as splendid persons. Shame results from a disparity between the ideal self and the real self; the greater the disparity, the greater the shame.

Conscience And Ideal Self. Conscience is the adult envelope of early moral training, focusing on what is right and what is wrong. It is the "judge" within, not your "chummy" sort of friend. The ideal self, on the other hand, seems more "friendly." It is deceptively innocuous on first glance. After all, what could be so bad about trying harder? What is wrong with setting high goals? Why not "shoot for the stars"?

Usually it is the **ideal self**, not the conscience, that is the culprit in problems of shame. As we noted already, conscience leads to guilt, which in turn invites confession, forgiveness, and growth; but failure to meet the expectations of the ideal self produces shame, which seldom fosters growth. It is precisely here that Christians frequently produce more problems than they heal. Much Christian preaching, writing, and dogma is concerned with raising the ideal self to ever higher levels. Unfortunately, this increases the disparity between the real and ideal selves, producing more shame. The irony is that by attempting to produce better, kinder, purer people, the Christian church has produced more shameful people!

The Grandiose Self. Clinicians (e.g., Jacobson, 1964) writing about shame refer to "narcissistic omnipotence," "grandiose self-representation," or to the "omnipotent self." Broucek (1982), for example, suggests that the words "haughty grandiosity," "shyness," and "feelings of inferiority" are all variants of shame. In one form or another, these all refer to an inflated ideal self; an ideal self that strives to be "perfect," an ideal self that cannot be satisfied with "good enough." Such perfectionism inflates the ideal self to gargantuan proportions, and the Christian church may unwittingly participate in the process.

The Xerox Syndrome. In many Sunday schools and parochial elementary schools, children are taught to copy Jesus as the perfect pattern. The prospect of eliminating the disparity between the ideal self and the real self when the ideal self is a Xerox of Jesus is dim indeed! It is bitterly ironic that in attempting to eliminate sin, Christians have set up a goal which echoes the original temptation, fall, and **shame** of humankind:

> *"You will not surely die," the serpent said to the woman, "for God knows that when you eat of it your eyes will be opened, and you will be like God, knowing good and evil."*
> *When the woman saw that the fruit of the tree was good for food and pleasing to the eye, and also desirable for gaining wisdom, she took some and ate it. She also gave some to her husband, who was with her, and he ate it. Then the eyes of both of them were opened, and they realized they were naked; so they sewed fig leaves together and made coverings for themselves.* (Genesis 3:4-8)

It is in attempting to be "like God" that we generate the highest levels of shame. The first recorded instances of shame occurred immediately following humankind's attempt to move into the realm of Godlikeness. Is it really much different today? Can the attempt to Xerox Jesus into the psyches of our children bring anything but shame? I do not think so. What I am suggesting is a radically different approach to the gospel.

The real gospel (good news) is "While we were still sinners, Christ died for us" (Romans 5:8). This corresponds to what Rogers (1959) termed unconditional positive regard. There is no hint of performance to gain acceptance. No copycat modeling of Jesus, no attempt at Christ cloning. Instead, there seems to be an acceptance of our fallen human state and a realization that salvation comes from without — from above. No psychological bootstrapping to improve the self, no constant striving to become more perfect — more "like Jesus."

Good-Enough Living. The English psychoanalyst Winnicott is largely responsible for the refreshing concept of "good-enough" mothering (1975). While other professionals were fastidiously suggesting ways in which mothers fail, and ways in which they might

89

improve, Winnicott maintained that mothers could be trusted and that they did not have to be perfect:

> *If it be true or even possible that the mental health of every individual is founded by the mother in her living experience with her infant, doctors and nurses can make it their first duty not to interfere. Instead of trying to teach mothers how to do what in fact cannot be taught, paediatricians must come sooner or later to recognize a good mother when they see one and then make sure that she gets full opportunity to grow to her job; mistakes she may, and indeed will, make, but if by these she becomes able to do better in subsequent attempts there is in the end a gain.*
> (Winnicott, 1975, pp. 161, 162)

Jesus And Good-Enough Living. Winnicott's notion is specifically relevant to understanding shame, and broadly applicable to Christian living in general. It was the Pharisees, not Jesus, who were the perfectionists of their day. But, some might point out, it was Jesus who said, "Be perfect, therefore, as your heavenly Father is perfect" (Matthew 5:48). Indeed, these were the words of our Lord, but they were not a call to perfectionism or scrupulosity. The original Greek word *telios*, here translated "perfect," really means "mature" or "complete" rather than flawless or error free. Jesus was suggesting that we ought to be mature and thorough in our earthly sphere, as the Father is wholesome and complete in His heavenly sphere.

The context supports such an exegesis. Jesus had just challenged His listeners to a high level of caring for other human beings. He encouraged them to love not only their friends, but also those unsavory sorts they had been prone to despise. This was, no doubt, an invitation to the most unselfish kind of life, but the emphasis was on interpersonal and social kindness, not on making one's life a photostatic copy of the Master.

Our obsession with cloning Jesus into our psyches creates a grandiose self and much shame, but little else. Such perfectionistic strivings create distance between us and our peers. We are likely to become obsessively introspective in searching to root out personal flaws, or we may become so concerned with "higher things" that we fail to be as the yeast or salt of Christ's parables — changing the world by permeating it with our presence.

Blueprint Or Inspiration? When believers stop trying to copy exactly Jesus' life they will then be able to develop more realistic ideal selves. This in no way reduces the importance of Christ as inspiration, but suggests relating to Him in a different way. The golfer who determines to precisely replicate the playing of Jack Nicklaus or Greg Norman will seldom enjoy a single round of the game. He or she will shamefully "fail" on most of the eighteen holes. If, instead, the golfer tries to play well, taking into account that 85 is the best game he or she has ever played, then he or she can be quite pleased to play bogey golf with an occasional par thrown in — inspired by Jack Nicklaus, rather than obsessed with copying him.

Such an attitude toward the example of Jesus might serve to reduce shame. Christians could retain Jesus Christ as the central inspiring figure/model of how to live the good life, just as golfers might see in Jack Nicklaus a model for how to play the game. This could be done without compulsively copying — or attempting to become a clone of the model.

The attempt to use Jesus as a blueprint results in all sorts of distorted conceptualizations of "goodness," including taking the vows of celibacy and poverty in a literalistic attempt to follow Jesus. Clearly, Jesus, as a bachelor, with a special mission, doesn't provide a literal blueprint for heterosexual relationships. However, his empathetic listening, his kindness to women and children, illustrate psychological essentials that can enhance all relationships — heterosexual as well as nonsexual.

PR — Personal Record — Instead Of Grandiosity. Another shame-reducing idea comes from the world of runners. A few years back, when children ran footraces in the schoolyard, there was always a single winner of the race, but this concept has become obsolete in an era when thousands of persons participate in a single race. In the strictest definition of the word, there is still a single winner of the New York Marathon, but that fails to account for age and sex differences. Consequently, race officials pass out trophies

91

to the fastest males and females in each age category, as well as for the entire field. More importantly, most of the fifteen or twenty thousand runners compete with themselves, trying to achieve a "PR" (personal record). For many — running their first marathon — this simply means completing the 26.2 miles without injury. If it takes five or six hours, no matter. Other more experienced runners attempt to better their previous marathon times, trying this time to run it in less than three hours, or in under five. And so it goes, each runner setting appropriate personal goals and measuring success according to that.

Such an attitude seems relevant to Christians, whatever form of exercise they choose. Early in his career the impassioned Paul asked the Corinthians: "Do you not know that in a race all the runners run, but only one gets the prize?" He then advised them: "Run in such a way as to get the prize" (1 Corinthians 9:24). This was a catch-22 because it could only have been attained by one of his listeners! Toward the end of his remarkable career the intrepid apostle offered a much more balanced attitude: "I have fought the good fight, I have finished the race, I have kept the faith" (2 Timothy 4:7).

The existential choice seems to be either to humanize the ideal self, or to experience psychological maladjustment. Without a realistic and humanized ideal self, Christians risk becoming dysfunctional. Most practicing clinicians encounter obsessive compulsive persons who neurotically strive to attain perfection. Others work with psychotic persons who generate paranoid delusions about being perfect — even confusing their identity with Jesus, the Pope, Moses, or some other perfect one. Yet another tack is illustrated by religious sociopaths — persons who circumvent the ideal self in their personal lives while vigorously promoting it as a necessity for others.

What is common to all the above cases — obsessive, paranoid, or sociopathic — is that whenever the ideal self is too perfectionistic, individuals resort to aberrant attempts to narrow the gap between the ideal self and the real self. A more viable alternative is to endeavor to become a better **human** instead of attempting to copy God.

Biblical Humanism vs. Secular Humanism. The defining characteristic of a Bible-based humanism is that it maintains the creatureliness of humankind *vis-a-vis* the divinity of Almighty God. Secular humanism, on the other hand, proposes a kind of god-within-the-person model. It sees goodness and truth emanating from within the person, and presumes that humans are capable of knowing what is best in the long run. When Adam and Eve, like secular humanists, aspired to find ultimate wisdom within themselves, they got into trouble. By abandoning their basic creatureliness, by trying to become totally self-sufficient, they were deceived into thinking themselves wise enough to shape their own destinies apart from God. Secular humanists still seek to rely primarily on themselves.

Maslow (1970), one of the founders of humanistic psychology, speculated about an ideal society which he dubbed "Eupsychia," meaning "good-mind country." Maslow believed that, left to themselves, people would make good choices, as illustrated in the following excerpt:

> *What kind of education would they choose? Economic system? Sexuality? Religion?*
>
> *I am very uncertain of some things — economics in particular. But of other things I am **very** sure. One of them is that this would almost surely be a (philosophically) anarchistic group, a Taoistic [nature-oriented] but loving culture, in which people (young people too) would have much more free choice than we are used to, and in which basic needs and metaneeds would be respected much more than they are in our society. People would not bother each other so much as we do, would be much less prone to press opinions or religions or philosophies or tastes in clothes or food or art or women on their neighbors. In a word, the inhabitants of Eupsychia would tend to be more Taoistic, nonintrusive, and basic need-gratifying (whenever possible), would frustrate only under certain conditions that I have not attempted to describe, would be more honest with each other than we are, and would permit people to make free choices wherever possible. They would be far less controlling, violent, contemptuous, or overbearing than we are. Under such conditions the deepest*

93

layers of human nature could show themselves with greater ease. (Maslow, 1970, pp. 277-278)

Such a description gives historians and other students of human behavior pause. Many would not trust that a society encouraging easy expression of the "deepest layers of human nature," would turn out to be consistent with Maslow's projections. Interestingly, he did not suggest under what conditions such a society would allow one member to "frustrate" another. Would there be no police? No taxes? No violence? Just as Skinner (1948) remained silent on who reinforced the reinforcers of his behavioristic utopia Walden II, Maslow leaves us with an idyllic fantasy that few could take seriously in the light of history. Eupsychia remains more a metaphor of what we wish human nature were like than what history shows it to be.

Adam And Eve: Models For Biblical Humanism

I have pointed out the futility of either "scrupulously copying Jesus" on the one hand, or following secular humanists by "looking within oneself" for ultimate values. There is another alternative. We can seek to reclaim our **pre-fall humanity**. The goal of the biblical humanist is to catch a glimpse of the humanism God intended when he created Adam and Eve.

Adam and Eve provide user-friendly models to emulate even while the biblical narrative of the fall exposes the primal precariousness of human wisdom and reminds us of the vulnerability of our creatureliness. On the positive side, we can imagine the Eden honeymooners joyfully blurring boundaries between work and play, finding their "work" so enriching and pleasant that "living for the weekend" was unknown to them. They originated recreational sex, naturally blending fun, love, caring, and procreation.

By contrast, scripture is conspicuously silent regarding Christ's erotic needs. This silence has been used to justify various monastic orders in which celibacy and poverty are (mistakenly, I think) cultivated in order to follow Jesus more devotedly.

Women find in Eve a model with which they comfortably identify. Though scriptures often report human activities occurring

94

in male-dominated cultures, this was not part of the original plan. Women who have been disenfranchised by sexist religionists may find congruence for themselves by identifying with Eve, or Miriam, or with Deborah the judge, instead of with Old Testament patriarchs.

Numerous other biblical superstars provide ample materials for a "good enough" instead of "perfect" **ideal self**. Noah erected a seaworthy monument to his faith, though later he became intoxicated and lay naked in his tent. Joseph became second in command over all of Egypt, although he began as the spoiled, bragging child of a doting father. Young David heroically slew the giant, but also commandeered his trusted general's wife, though he had haremsful from which to choose. Moses patiently herded a grumbling nation of slaves through walls of water and seas of sand into a land dominated by giants. En route, he even participated in a summit conference with Yahweh. Nonetheless, before he realized his goal of marching into the promised land, he "lost it" (his temper, and with it the opportunity to finish his long trek).

Clones, Copycats, Or Children?

In summary, this is not a call for moral flabbiness or ethical apathy. On the contrary, biblical humanism calls us to "self-actualization" of the highest sort, to the fullest pursuit of our potential; but this is always within the context of our creatureliness. Our search is not for self-sufficiency or for a new-age god within, but for restoration to our unfallen potential as sons and daughters of the Almighty Creator. Such biblical humanism is grounded in the understanding that we were originally created in His image — not as clones, not as copycats, but as His children:

> Let us make man in our image, in our likeness ... So God created man in his own image, in the image of God he created him; male and female he created them. (Genesis 1:26, 27)

Christians seeking to reclaim their lost humanity are on firm psychological and theological ground. They can avoid secular humanism's search for god within on the one hand, and perfectionistic mimicry of Jesus on the other. Instead, they may joyfully celebrate their humanity, seeking to restore in themselves and others a bit of paradise lost. Such humanism can help break the shame-generating cycles created by well-intended but misguided efforts to become Jesus clones. Thinking of Adam and Eve in their unfallen happiness will provide appropriate models that are less likely to generate shame and more likely to affirm and encourage.

Christians might well join Adam in celebrating Eve's humanity with *joie de vivre*:

> *This is now bone of my bones*
> *and flesh of my flesh;*
> *she shall be called woman,*
> *for she was taken out of man.*
>   *For this reason a man will leave his father and mother*
> *and be united to his wife, and they will become one flesh.*
>   *The man and his wife were both naked, and they felt no*
> *shame.* (Genesis 2:23-25)

How Striving-To-Be-Perfect People Forgive

In this chapter we've seen how the seemingly commendable goal of "trying to be like Christ" can backfire, causing unnecessary shame for the person and making it almost impossible to forgive. This failure to forgive oneself for being human makes it almost impossible genuinely to forgive others for their mistakes. Forgiveness — like water — seeks its own level; if you can't forgive yourself for being less than perfect, you will find it impossible to forgive the shortcomings of others. This is why the Pharisees and other moralistic perfectionists have always had such a hard time with mercy. The Pharisees found Christ's eagerness to forgive not only puzzling, but downright scandalous. Their obsessive attempts to become flawless eclipsed the larger picture of mercy and forgiveness that Christ embodied.

Chapter 7

How *Personality Styles* Influence Forgiveness

(Potpourri Of Styles)

In a previous chapter we studied the histrionic and obsessive-compulsive styles in considerable detail, but I don't want to leave you with the impression that psychological styles are homogeneous or that they exist with clear-cut boundaries in the real world. They are, rather, broad outlines, providing a general orientation to psychological styles of thinking and handling emotions. Furthermore, there are no "pure" styles to be found in the real world. Rather, people have "streaks" of various styles in their personalities. So before we go further, let's take a few moments to understand how style appears in the real world.

Personality Styles And Yogurt Dispensers
Think of your personality as a yogurt dispenser — you know, the kind you see with four flavors and the capacity to swirl two of the flavors together. But think of personality as a yogurt dispenser capable of a swirling together a dozen different flavors (**styles**). We've examined two major "flavors" and I will briefly mention additional kinds, but keep in mind that what you'll encounter in real life will be a "swirled rainbow" of different styles in varying proportions — all in the same person. And of course, your **religious** style is only one expression of your total personality style.

Is there an ideal religious style? Just as in daily life, where balance and flexibility are the hallmarks of health, so in the spiritual realm, the best style is a **balanced** combination of thinking *and* feeling. It is in rigidly clinging to either extreme that the obsessive or the hysteric appears pathological. Recall that in the parable of the soils, the gospel seed deposited in "rocky" (histrionic)

97

places sprang up quickly, but lacked roots, while other plants were choked by "thorns" (obsessive-compulsive "worries of this life"). Jesus characterized good soil as a balanced blend of enthusiastic feeling and careful thinking:

> *But the one who received the seed that fell on good soil is the man who* **hears** *the word* **and understands** *it. He produces a crop, yielding a hundred, sixty or thirty times what was sown.* (Matthew 13:23) [bold face mine]

In other passages we also see this same balance. To the obsessive-compulsive worriers of His day Jesus soothingly suggested:

> *Therefore I tell you, do not worry about your life, what you will eat or drink; or about your body, what you will wear. Is not life more important than food, and the body more important than clothes? Look at the birds of the air; they do not sow or reap or store away in barns, and yet your heavenly Father feeds them. Are you not much more valuable than they? Who of you by worrying can add a single hour to his life?*
> *And why do you worry about clothes? See how the lilies of the field grow. They do not labor or spin. Yet I tell you that not even Solomon in all his splendor was dressed like one of these. If that is how God clothes the grass of the field, which is here today and tomorrow is thrown into the fire, will he not much more clothe you?* (Matthew 6:25-30)

Notice, however, in sowing the gospel seed among the obsessive, worrying "thorns," Jesus is soothingly reassuring — not condemning. He suggests that His listeners have no reason to worry because the Father cares for all creatures — even those incapable of worrying. Jesus' style was to foster balance by providing soothing reassurance:

> *Are not two sparrows sold for a penny? Yet not one of them will fall to the ground apart from the will of your Father. And* **even the very hairs of your head are all**

numbered. So don't be afraid; you are worth more than many sparrows. (Matthew 10:29-31) [bold face mine]

What could be more reassuring to obsessive-compulsive worriers than to be told that the hairs of their heads were *already counted!* By the Father! In today's parlance:

"Hey, guys! Your compulsive counting is unnecessary, my Dad's got it all under control. Relax!" We know however, that reassurance does not instantly bring balance into an obsessive-compulsive lifestyle. Nonetheless, it provides existential "soil" for reconsidering one's frantic attempts to control everything.

Grass Seed And Gospel Seed. Perhaps the lesson of the parable is not so much that certain kinds of soil are good and others are bad, but rather that a wise sower blends his seeds to fit particular areas of the lawn. You plant a different blend of grass seed in shady areas than you do where sunlight is direct. Jesus — the sage sower — was a genius at blending seed. He was exquisitely attuned to the needs of those around him and empathically dispensed just the right blend of gospel seeds.

To obsessive-compulsives He said, "I've already got it counted." But for histrionics who are inclined *only* to trust and *feel* good, He told the parable of the talents (Matthew 25) extolling the virtues of hard work. However, just in case obsessive-compulsives might grab onto that to justify their workaholic styles, He also told the parable of the workers in the vineyard (Matthew 20), showing that work is not an end in itself, and that the Father rewards His workers in ways that do not follow rigid formulas. If the Father chose to pay a worker who worked an hour from four to five the same as someone who had worked from eight to five, it was no big deal — nothing to obsess about.

Blended Forgiveness

The application to forgiving seems clear. Forgiveness ought to be individually blended to meet the unique needs of the forgiven. Like spices used in cooking, or medications used in healing, careful thought ought to go into the forgiveness recipe. This is not something where "one size fits all." Histrionics need to *feel* forgiven, whereas obsessives need to *know* that their moral account is *balanced*!

Forgiving styles, like the personality styles that undergird them, come in varying **combinations** — rainbow-flavored yogurt. Such stylistic "streaks" vary considerably from person to person. One human "sundae" might be mostly purple, another predominantly orange, while still another might be evenly swirled among several flavors. Even when you can discern a dominant streak (**style**), boundaries among the streaks are, like in the rainbow itself, not precisely delineated. Like differences between twilight and darkness or dawn and daylight, colors merge into one another. Consequently, you can never exactly pigeonhole people on the basis of style, nor can your forgiveness blend be perfect. Nonetheless, as you understand others better, your ability to relate mercifully and with compassion will increase.

Like an experienced collector of fine art or antiques, you'll be more sensitive in knowing what to look for. You'll relate more easily to persons with differing psychological styles. This won't always be easy, but since persons are more valuable than antiques or art pieces, your effort to understand these human "yogurt dispensers" will be an excellent investment, rewarded with a deeper understanding of personal styles and better understanding of each person's experiences in forgiving and being forgiven.

More Styles

Shame-permeated people dispense **"Of-course!" forgiveness**. Shameful believers are distinguished by excessive "humility" (read "psychological insecurity"). They expend inordinate efforts *seeking* forgiveness for themselves. Mired in their own sense of inferiority, they constantly feel the need not only of affirmation, but of amnesty. Consequently, when someone asks *them* for forgiveness, it comes as a surprise and almost an honor that someone would consider them important enough to care whether or not they would dispense a bit of pardon.

Shame is the HIV of the soul. The "carrier" is often unaware that this virulent virus is at work destroying love, joy, peace, patience, kindness, gentleness, self-confidence, and other such "fruits" of a healthy spirit. Usually the victim is only aware of being trapped in a perfection-shame cycle where shame is the result of failing to achieve perfection, and is the fuel that drives perfectionistic striving even more intensely. The hymn that begins, "Alas and did my Savior die ... for such a worm as I," is an appropriate elegy for such a person's self-image.

As you'll recall from the first chapter, people with self-esteem difficulties find it difficult to forgive either themselves or others. What passes as forgiveness is really shame and insecurity. "Of course I'll forgive you," they might say outwardly while adding the inward, "I'm just a worm, I deserved to be mistreated in the first place, so it's not a big deal to forgive you." With these people you hardly have to ask for pardon, because they've already acquitted you with their own inferiority. In transactional analysis terms: "You're OK; I'm not OK."

Dependent people dispense "Please-like-me" forgiveness. So fragile is their own autonomy and security that they long for someone upon whom they can depend. Less severely despising of themselves than the shameful, they nonetheless have many of the same tendencies. For them forgiveness is a way of bribing you into liking them. Of course they'll forgive, if only you'll become a pal in return. Theologically they make a talisman of verses like "Cast all your anxiety on him because he cares for you" (1 Peter 5:7). Their favorite hymn might be "Oh Safe to the Rock that is higher than I."

Co-dependent forgivers build their lives around turning the other cheek or going the second mile. These people — often from alcoholic or abusive families — have usually spent their childhood years being "little adults." Sometimes known as **parental** or **parentified** children, they spend their time vigilantly caring for other family members instead of playing with friends and enjoying their early years.

Subconsciously they are always humming the hymn "I Surrender All," and subsequently they often grow up to marry alcoholic, sociopathic, or otherwise abusive spouses. Tragically, they tend to sustain the very problems they hope to eliminate by their kindness. A famous psychiatrist, who spent years working with troubled youth, once wrote a book entitled *Love Is Not Enough*, suggesting that compassion, even when coupled with the best of intentions, isn't enough to break destructive cycles of behavior. This is certainly true in the case of co-dependent personalities. They "care," often very deeply, but this very caring makes it possible for the pathology to continue.

In our present discussion we can say that they "forgive" even when such behavior reinforces the pathology of a perpetrator. Their problems of low self-esteem mesh perfectly with someone else's need to dominate, so they often find themselves in an abuse cycle which is extremely difficult to break because "forgiveness" becomes the epoxy holding together complementary neuroses.

In many spouse-abuse cycles, for example the co-dependent's "forgiveness" allows the cycle to continue. Typically such cycles begin with a gradual build-up of unspoken anger in the assaulter. (Such spouses are notoriously inept at **nonviolently verbalizing** their anger.) The mate experiences the steady build-up of the spouse's anger, but fear-based attempts to placate the anger only exacerbate the imminent attack. When the attack finally occurs, the assaulted spouse experiences immediate helplessness, shame, and humiliation, whereas the assaulter feels a temporary "burst" of relief and a sense of power.

In the calm that follows the violence, a gradual but powerful reversal begins to take place. The assaulter becomes increasingly ashamed, embarrassed, and even powerless — especially if the spouse presses charges. The victimized spouse grows to feel more powerful and this is often reinforced by the now-contrite mate who promises this will never happen again. Toch (1969) describes the experience of assaulted women in the hospital:

> *Within a few days they went from being lonely, angry, frightened, and hurt to being happy, confident, and loving ... These women were thoroughly convinced of their desire to stop being victims, until the batterer arrived. I always knew when a woman's husband had made contact with her by the profusion of flowers, candy, cards and other gifts in her hospital room.* (p. 66)

Co-dependent "forgiveness" is fool's gold, it sparkles on the outside but lacks true value. What appears as forgiveness is really psychological insecurity.

102

Manipulative/slick persons seem to have "radar" for co-dependents and are often found in the role of "perpetrator." Such people, sometimes known as **sociopaths** or **antisocial personalities**, are characterized by their failure to keep promises, sexual promiscuity, inconsistent work history, harassing, stealing, lying, or engaging in illegal activities. However, even when such blatantly unacceptable behaviors are not evident, manipulative/slick people fail to feel remorse when they've hurt others, use words primarily to exploit (rather than communicate with) others, and use relationships to gratify themselves.

Although they are terribly destructive, they are usually not the hatchet-wielding serial killers shown in movies. Rather, in ordinary life, they are con artists, and we often find a "streak" of sociopathy in successful salesmen, politicians, and televangelists. Obviously, not all manipulative people are destructive or engage in criminal behavior. In fact, in highly competitive careers such as business, sales, law, or politics, a bit of slickness is sometimes an asset in getting to the top. The terms "Tricky Dicky" and "Slick Willy" illustrate the point.

Needless to say, such people are not good partners in any kind of long-term relationship whether it involves business or friendship. And a rule of thumb when encountering them is "actions speak louder than words." She may be charming and gifted in words and promises, she may be a captivating conversationalist, but her *behavior,* which is traitorous over time, nullifies her words. He's the kind of guy who sends you a dozen long-stem roses while having an affair with your best friend. He knows how to "say it with flowers," but he lacks loyalty.

Words from manipulative/slick people are like the checks they write, which often come back marked "insufficient funds." When such people say, "I care about you," beware! This really means: "Trust me, so that I can exploit you for my own purposes." When they use words like love or trust, they have an entirely different meaning from what you've come to expect. Like bad checks which aren't backed with cash, they can never be trusted. For them life is a giant Scrabble game or crossword puzzle where words are carefully arranged to win points or fill in blank spaces, but where their use is decided only by the needs of the moment.

Although they *talk* about trust as a way of manipulating others, they are neither trustworthy nor trusting. Their not-so-golden rule is "Do unto others, *before* they do to you!" They're highly impulsive, trust only themselves, have few loyalties, are glib with words, and experience little remorse. "*C'est la vie*" is as close as they come to saying "I'm sorry."

We're prone to believe "All's fair in love and war," "business is business," "finders keepers, losers weepers," or "it's just politics." We *expect* our politicians to lie, our movie stars to be involved in numerous superficial sexual relationships, and business persons to live by the "bottom line." They seldom disappoint us. Yet, since we want so badly to idealize something or someone, we tried to believe Nixon when he said "I'm no crook," or Clinton when he declared, "I didn't inhale."

Now that you're acquainted with some traits of the exploitive/slick person, will you be able to avoid being misused? I hope so, but it won't be easy, because she's so good at making you feel that *you*, not *she*, is the center of her world. His honeyed words disguise his search for immediate gratification. Most importantly, remember when he says "I promise," or "I'm sorry," or "I'll never do that again," these are *only* words — empty words — bad checks.

Bottom line: *Don't* "forgive" manipulative/slick (sociopathic) persons. It only reinforces their exploiting. *Don't* turn the other cheek. *Don't* go the second mile. This is where you must *not* forgive "seventy times seven." Although religiously-sophisticated sociopaths will sometimes quote scripture while trying to exploit you, this is one kind of person for whom "seventy times seven" does *not* apply.

Forgiveness from a sociopath is worth nothing! Forgiveness offered to a sociopath is probably a symptom of sickness on your part. Sounds harsh, but sociopaths merely exploit your generosity and *do not* change as a result of being "forgiven." Worse yet, as we saw in the case of the spouse-abuse cycle, such "forgiveness" is processed by them as **reinforcement**. They are *less* likely to change for the better when forgiven and *more* likely to go on hurting others and themselves.

Put in religious terms: forgiveness has no redemptive value for the sociopath. Thus, "going the second mile" or "turning the other cheek" is harmful rather than beneficial for both the sociopath and the victim. When interacting with a sociopath, we do well to recall Christ's words to his disciples before sending them out to work are apropos: "I am sending you out like sheep among wolves. Therefore be as shrewd as snakes and as innocent as doves" (Matthew 10:16).

Narcissistic persons find it difficult to forgive and almost never request forgiveness. "Forgiveness" from narcissists doesn't feel like forgiveness at all. In fact, it feels like you hurt them almost beyond repair, but if you really go out of your way to admire them, they might be able to "forgive" you. Narcissists constantly seek reassurance that they are "special." Because of a profound sense of inner emptiness, they require admiration as most people require oxygen — almost constantly. They crave adoration so intensely and at such high levels that they feel "slighted" or "ignored" by normal levels of friendship. Trying to ward off inner emptiness by cultivating external adoration, they sometimes appear grandiose in their self-esteem. It's as if they don't discern the difference between singing "He's got the *whole world* in his hand" and "He's gotta you and *me*, brother, in his hand." In his heart, he's really singing "He's got ... *me,* brother, in his hand."

Like histrionics, narcissists seek attention, are often sexually seductive, and are overly concerned with physical attractiveness. But they seek more than mere attention; they incessantly seek to capture your admiration. They are **compulsive** not about washing their hands, counting cracks in the sidewalk, or other rituals, but rather about gaining your adoration. "*I must be special to you!*" is the narcissist's core compulsion. They appear to have a grandiose sense of self-importance, exaggerating their accomplishments and talents in order to be noticed as special. When adequately stroked or flattered, they respond with charm and effervescence — almost purring — but when criticized they react outwardly with feelings of outrage and inwardly with shame.

Like histrionics, they are emotionally intense but psychologically shallow, loving the limelight and craving adoration. Like obsessives they seek perfection and achievement; but different from obsessives, they *don't* feel they have to earn it or work for it. Rather, they are *entitled* to admiration. In this way they are similar to the manipulative/slick people we've just considered, who also have an unrealistic sense of entitlement. Narcissists see themselves as special, elite, a cut above the common folks who have to earn admiration through achievement. Often they're preoccupied — as much of our culture seems to be — with the rich and the famous, sometimes developing elaborate fantasy relationships with other "special" people such as movie stars or important political figures.

Envy and **disdain** are the poles of the narcissistic person's world. Others are either put up on a pedestal and admired (as the narcissist wishes to be admired) or disdained as below social worthiness. Narcissists live suspended between movie stars and street people, between Hollywood and hobos. They try to come off as stars, but secretly fear they're bums.

There is a country western song written and recorded by Mac Davis which captures the veneer of vainness seen in narcissistic lovers, but also hints at the inner emptiness:

It's Hard To Be Humble

Oh, Lord, it's hard to be humble,
When you're perfect in every way.
I can't wait to look in the mirror,
'Cause I get better lookin' each day.
To know me is to love me,
I must be a helluva man.
Oh, Lord, it's hard to be humble,
But I'm doin' the best that I can.

I used to have a girlfriend,
But I guess she just couldn't compete,
With all these love-starved women
Who keep clambering at my feet.
Well, I probably could find me another,
But I guess they're all in awe of me.
Who cares, I never get lonesome,
'Cause I treasure my own company.

I guess you could say I'm a loner,
A cowboy outlaw tough and proud,
Well, I could have lots of friends if I wanted,
But then I wouldn't stand out from the crowd.
Some folks say that I'm egotistical,
Hell, I don't even know what that means.
I guess it has something to do with the way that
I fill out my skin-tight blue jeans.

Oh, Lord, it's hard to be humble
When you're perfect in every way.
I can't wait to look in the mirror,
'Cause I get better lookin' each day.
To know me is to love me,
I must be a helluva man.
Oh, Lord, it's hard to be humble,
But I'm doin' the best that I can.

(Used by permission)

"Thank you" and "I'm sorry" are words that a narcissist finds almost impossible to utter. This is because narcissists desperately attempt to protect their fragile sense of self by living an illusion — the illusion of **needlessness** and **perfection**. In their interactions they attempt to be needless and sinless — self-sufficient and perfect — obviating the necessity to say, "Thank you" or "I'm sorry."

When a narcissistic person says, "I'm sorry," it may at first sound like a genuine apology. But it soon becomes apparent that what is really occurring is not an attempt at repairing a breached relationship. The narcissist is really seeking to restore his **own illusion of perfection** by fixing things — often in indirect ways. This is what psychoanalysts refer to as **undoing**.

For example, a wife who has hurt her husband may cook him a special dinner or signal her availability for sexual intercourse — all without having to say those impossible words "I'm sorry." The narcissistic husband who has offended his wife brings flowers *instead* of apologizing. The narcissistic parent who insensitively hurts her child's feelings offers a treat in place of "I'm sorry."

In all such cases, narcissists attempt to undo damage without apologizing. But such counterfeit contrition only worsens the relationship, because the injured person is made to feel guilty for not being more forgiving to a person who is supposedly sorry, and the narcissistic person feels resentful that the undoing gifts are not more appreciated.

Narcissists avoid authentic apologies by appealing to good intentions. "I really meant to stop by and see you while you were in the hospital, but I couldn't get away from my Little League coaching during visiting hours." Such *apparent* apologies really amount to self-justification.

Real apologies are based on **empathy** for the injured person's pain, regardless of whether the pain was intentionally or accidentally inflicted, but empathy isn't part of the narcissistic person's emotional repertoire. Narcissistic "apologies" are designed primarily to emphasize the narcissist's faultlessness, and to make him **appear** genuinely concerned about the suffering of another. When the narcissist "apologizes" by saying, "I'm sorry I was late, you would not believe the traffic — what a pain to get here!" he often sounds irritated, and instead of communicating genuine remorse or empathy, he makes the other person feel as if **he** has done something wrong by worrying.

Explaining instead of apologizing is how narcissists go through the motions of asking "forgiveness." Typical explanations *sans* apology take the form of "I must have forgotten your birthday because my mother was in the hospital." Such apologies are designed to elicit sympathy for narcissists rather than to express genuine regret over hurt they might have caused.

I once heard a co-worker, sophisticated in psychological theories, "apologize" to our office manager: "Gee, I must have been feeling unconsciously irritated with you when I blew up, because you reminded me of my aunt, who was always on my case when I was growing up. Sorry about that."

A woman I know is married to a narcissistic social worker who labels her a "masochist" whenever she brings up a problem in their marriage.

So much for various styles of forgiving. I trust you realize this is only a taste. Although we've examined the histrionic and obsessive styles in depth, it's simply beyond the scope of this book to discuss carefully a dozen different personality styles in such detail. For our present purposes, it suffices to realize that **forgiveness** has many different expressions, which are shaped by the personality style of the forgiver and colored by the personality style of the forgiven.

Summary

We have seen how psychological and religious behaviors comingle in the process of forgiving. We have learned that although personality style is extremely complex and is influenced by numerous factors, yet there is a discernable consistency in each style. Human behavior always reflects an interaction between the numerous factors outside ourselves (situation) and our inner personality styles. Additionally, when we speak of things theological, complexity increases because we must allow for the working of the Spirit and other influences which cannot be studied utilizing the scientific method.

Furthermore, in exploring the spiritual life, we are faced not only with the complexities of palpable human behavior but also with the existential mysteries of The Almighty, clothed in enigmas intrinsic to divinity and clouded by ambiguities intrinsic to human communication. Surely then, our deepest insights exist only as embryos. Always we are destined to "see through a glass darkly," and no amount of psychological or theological theory can change that.

Yet, since we were destined for dialogue with the Divine, designed — like Jacob it seems — to grapple with Jehovah, we must continue to try. Though we're told, "His ways are past finding out," we still attempt to reach out. Though it seems arrogant to seek encounter with the Mighty One of Israel — Who allowed His trusted servant Moses only a glimpse of His backside — we seem compelled to continue. And though the Christ of the Gospels seems more "user-friendly," He is, after all, the one who turned water into wine, raised people from the dead, and burst the tomb on that Easter morning. Hardly the subject for an ordinary psychoanalysis.

This is why I have chosen to emphasize the **psychology** of forgiveness more than theology, because if we can more accurately understand human styles of functioning, it will enable us to forgive with empathy. I'm willing to trust existential and salvation issues to the Father. Also, of course, I'm a psychologist, not a theologian, so I've tried to stay in my own area of expertise.

In the next chapter we will consider the cases of two courageous people in order to illustrate the healing power of forgiveness. The first case illustrates getting beyond abuses of the past by forgiving others. The second illustrates self-forgiveness in the form of letting go of mistakes of former years.

Chapter 8

Savannah And Kathleen

Savannah Lynn — A Case Study In Forgiving Others

Savannah Lynn was beautiful. Her dark chestnut hair lay over her shoulders with a thickness and hue that rivaled the manes of her father's prized thoroughbreds. Wide-set eyes, chiseled nose, and flawless skin all added to the appearance of "Southern aristocrat" in a peach taffeta dress. Sitting in my waiting room she looked as if she might have just arrived from Tara, or some other southern plantation, but when she stood up, I knew something was wrong. Terribly wrong.

"Hi, I'm Dr. Berecz. Please come in."

Sluggishly she began to emerge from the white wicker chair in the corner of my waiting room. It seemed like forever as she unfolded her waxily-stiff body up out of the chair. Finally standing, she was tall, towerlike, immobile. Mute and motionless, she could have been a graceful goddess on the back lawn of a luxurious plantation, hoisting aloft a bird bath with one arm, clutching ivy in her other hand. And it wasn't only how she looked; magnolia blossom perfume co-mingled with her Nieman-Marcus dress and exquisite jewelry to create a portrait of antebellum femininity seldom seen north of the Mason-Dixon line.

Slowly, comalike, she moved toward my office door, and as she did, my reverie was broken. I wasn't an extra on the set of *Gone with the Wind*; this was Michigan on a dreary February afternoon, and unbeknownst to me, I was about to begin one of the most remarkable journeys of my clinical career. Beneath this veneer of southern elegance and poise was a wreckage of terrorism and sexual abuse so terrible that it had split Savannah into five personalities. The flawless makeup and elegant clothing hid a "family" of frightened children so terrified they hardly dared move.

111

Inside my office, she warily scanned for seating options, choosing the farthest end of my leather couch. When Savannah finally answered my question, "What brings you here?" she spoke with a "drawl" that transformed efficient Yankee-clipped monosyllables into the polysyllabic musicality of the deep South. "I thought you could help me" became "Aaa ... eeh thaw ... oat yaw ... awl co ... ooed hay ... yelp maah ... eeh."

And so began my journey into a nightmare so monstrous it had split Savannah into several selves, each of whom relentlessly battled to keep all intruders away from the dark secrets which originally caused the splitting and remained to fuel the fires of her internal hell. Seething beneath her catatonic immobility were secrets so dark, abuses so awful, that no one person could have survived such ordeals, so Savannah had split up the work and now each alternate personality had a job to do. In this sense, Savannah was similar to other multiple personalities I had treated.

Fortunately, genuine cases of Multiple Personality (now known as Dissociative Identity Disorder) are rare, but when abuse is extremely severe, or a child too young to develop adequate coping mechanisms, the individual sometimes splits into several different personalities, with each personality responsible for protecting and preserving different parts of the child.

In another case, a woman who had been raped by her father and his friends when she was four years of age developed several **passive** personalities at the time of the rape because she learned that resistance only made the pain more severe.

In yet another case — a female who had also been raped by her father at a very early age — two **hostile** personalities developed. One was a little boy whose whole existence was focused on killing the father. The other was also a hostile boy, but he was centered on keeping the other boy's homicidal rage from exploding.

Another case study illustrates how personalities come into existence in order to **preserve** a part of the child which is threatened by the abuser. One little girl was musically talented and loved to play the piano; however, she refused to play anymore after her mother threatened to break her fingers if she made any more mistakes. She never played again in the presence of another person;

112

but an alternate personality was created to preserve her love of music and would play for hours when the little girl was entirely alone in the house. No other human being ever heard this little girl play music again.

All of us are "multiple personalities," living within one "self" on the golf course, another at the office, yet another at home. As we saw earlier, **situations** strongly influence our behavior, eliciting different selves on different occasions. Unlike Savannah's "family" of selves, however, our selves remain **co-conscious** and **coordinated** throughout all these varying circumstances. Even when I'm my "golf self" at the local course, I am conscious of my "therapist" self, "husband" self, and "father" self, and could easily transition into any one of them. Furthermore, I know that all these are part of the overall self known by others as John Berecz and by me as "I."

The primary differences between healthy "yogurt-dispenser" **blended** selves within one person and Savannah's **splitting** into completely different personalities is mostly a matter of degree, not kind. The multiple personality's selves are more rigid and isolated from each other than yours or mine, but multiple personalities are not entirely different from you or me. In this sense, Savannah's story is your story, my story. Most of us have been lucky enough to handle our troubles without developing deep splits within our selves, but Savannah's experiences were so terrible she could not.

In treating patients like Savannah, I have learned that the usual year or so of psychotherapy is only a beginning. In order to achieve a complete and lasting healing, it takes much longer.

So as I listened to Savannah's story, I knew it would be a long road ahead. I would have to gain the trust not only of Savannah, the executive personality, but also of each one of her "family" of selves — e.g., David, the strong male with a partially mutilated face who helped eight-year-old Savannah back to the house the night she was gang raped by Klansmen.

I would have to overcome the hostility of Clara, who would emerge with dry heaves, choking, and savage biting of her fingers which she would force into her mouth as a kind of proxy penis whenever memories of forced oral sex resurfaced. Clara frequently awoke in the night feeling suffocated and sexually aroused, wiping "blood" off her body, before realizing it was perspiration. Nights for Clara were horrifying as she relived the terrors of being raped by white-robed Klansmen. But not only was she in constant fear of these hooded rapists, she was regularly petrified into immobility by a masked intruder who once slipped into her bedroom at night. It was only years later, in therapy, that she recognized the intruder as a family member.

Jennifer was (to use Savannah's words) "a beautiful green hummingbird." Jennifer had watched from the branch of a tree that terrifying twilight when several Klansmen raped Clara. And just as dusk turned to darkness — a fitting metaphor of the horrible experience she had just witnessed — Jennifer turned into a wooden bird and never flew or sang again. In therapy she was a silent observer who never spoke, never wrote, but sometimes drew pictures.

The elegant "Southern Lady" I'd just met would be replaced by terrified children who would, during the course of the next several years, develop enough trust to come to therapy. Entering my waiting room I would find, instead of *Gone-with-the-Wind* elegance, a little girl huddled in the corner clutching a large stuffed animal, shivering with fear. Sometimes I would encounter a teen who was both terrified and truculent, ready to "walk out" of our session at the slightest misunderstanding. Or, even worse, I might find a **comatose** Charlotte, the personality who coped with terror by holding still. She would move with the kind of stiff, waxy flexibility usually seen only in catatonic schizophrenics or the profoundly depressed.

Each of these "persons within the person" carried out a life-sustaining function, each was absolutely necessary to Savannah's survival, but each carried out his or her business separately, which led to chaos within Savannah and turmoil within therapy.

Encountering her nearly two decades into my career, I had experienced "stormy" sessions with other clients, but I'd never been caught in the center of a tornado before. Never before had I been so violently hurled from emotion to emotion within a few short minutes.

114

Just as in the case of the little girl who developed an alternate self that continued to play the piano after her mother threatened to break her fingers, Savannah's selves were like lifeguards, created to rescue and resuscitate a little girl who nearly drowned in the riptide childhood trauma during her early formative years. Each of her personalities coped with specific aspects of the abuse, and by splitting up the work, they could handle it. No little girl could have handled all the trauma by herself.

I once heard psychotherapy defined as **re-parenting**, and there is no better description for the kind of work I carried out with Savannah. To her, after three or four years of twice/weekly psychotherapy, I finally became the safe parent she had never known.

She was, in the early therapy hours, a chaotic cauldron of inconsistencies. Frequently boiling with rage yet mute with terror, seething with resentment but whimpering with fear, Savannah and her alternates covered a spectrum of emotions with an intensity I'd never before seen contained within one person.

And, I suppose, Savannah *wasn't* one person when I met her that dreary February afternoon so long ago. But as our first moments together expanded into hours, weeks, months, years — finally, almost a decade of intensive psychotherapy — Savannah's self expanded to contain all the emotions that resulted from the innumerable episodes of terror, pain, and humiliation she suffered as a child, and she **integrated** into a cohesive person who no longer splits at the slightest indication of danger.

Savannah's story is the account of a little girl surviving the most awful kinds of mistreatment by ultimately forgiving (letting go) and moving on with her life. Its grisly details could easily occupy an entire book, but here I need only share enough to show you how she transcended the profundity of her pain and the magnitude of her terror with the miracle of forgiveness.

Savannah's father was a podiatrist who used his medical expertise not only in his professional office, but to implement the most nefarious schemes a father could perpetrate on his own child. Even worse, he never "owned" any of his abuse by directly fondling Savannah or openly making sexual overtures during the daylight hours. Instead, under cover of darkness, he cross-dressed, using lipstick, perfume, and various costumes to appear as a woman. This increased Savannah's terror tenfold.

Entering Savannah's bedroom at night, "Daddy in drag" carried out all manner of sexual perversions, using drugs to "relax" her. And these were not just occasional happenings. From the time Savannah was a child until she left home as a teenager, such episodes occurred several times each month.

And if that weren't enough agony for one child, sometime during early adolescence Savannah was gang raped by several Klansmen, whom she suspected were her father's friends.

Subsequently, she experienced horrible flashbacks. Once during a particularly painful recollection of these sordid events, Clara sobbingly wailed, "I used to think I saw angels in my room." Indeed, during flashbacks, she saw beings in white garb, but far from "angels," these evil men wore the sinister white robes of the KKK.

Little wonder that as an adult Savannah cycled between the comatose stiffness of catatonia and the dizzying activity of mania. Both replicated her experiences during the tragic traumas of childhood. She had learned to survive Daddy's night visits by "holding still" and she had tried to defend against the rape by "running like crazy."

In therapy she began to understand things which had never before made sense. For example, she often woke up dreaming she was being suffocated to the point of passing out and then being revived. As an adult medical professional herself, she now suspects that her sadistic father would suffocate her until she would lose consciousness and then revive her. As a child she only remembered feelings of suffocation and very sore ribs the next morning, which she suspects were sore because of CPR or artificial respiration procedures.

Since Daddy was a respected professional, a regular churchgoer, and esteemed member of the local community — he was the local mayor's personal podiatrist — Savannah knew that if she were to tell of these terrible nighttime happenings, no one would have believed her. In all likelihood *she* would have been punished, or at least accused of lying. Even after she grew to adulthood, became involved in psychotherapy, and gained the courage to confront her father, he typed the following letter on his professional stationery:

Dearest Savannah,

Happy birthday! It hardly seems possible that you're thirty-one! I know this must be a trying time for you, but I can only say that I have never touched any part of your body except to hug your waist or shoulders. I have never seen you nude. I have never seen your breasts or your pubic area. I have never had any sexual desires toward you, and am not sure if I have ever kissed you on the lips.

I had always felt we had a wonderful Father-Daughter relationship. I can scarcely understand what has gone wrong. You will always be a precious daughter to me and I hope through some reconciliation in the future we can resume our closeness.

Your mother and I are very proud of your accomplishments and hope that God will richly bless you this next year. Our prayers are for you and we wish for nothing but happiness and joy in your life. At least twice a day our prayers are for your welfare and happiness.

Love,
Dad

(Then a handwritten P.S. from her mother:) *I love you, Savannah, and always will. In spite of everything you've accused Dad of doing. Believe me, it isn't true. I'll never stop loving you and praying for you. Again Happy Birthday, darling.*
Mother

This was one of many such letters she received during the course of psychotherapy. All were of the same genre. All absolutely denied any wrongdoing, and all attested to deep parental love and a wish for God's blessings on her. You can just imagine that if such denial was the response to an adult woman in her thirties, a nine-year-old girl would have been totally discounted.

I'm not going to discuss this complex case in extensive detail. I refer to it (with Savannah's permission) in order to illustrate the transforming power of forgiveness, even in cases of unimaginable evil. You have enough information to understand the depth of

Savannah's trauma and the magnitude of her parents' denial. How then did she ever find it within herself to forgive such heinous evils?

The first step was to face her darkest secrets, her most horrifying terrors, and to realize that her very own father was the source of the diabolical evils carried out against her. It took several years for her to fully come to this conclusion.

Years of conditioning by her father, combined with threats of reprisals if she should confront the abuse, had left Savannah little choice but to collude with her parents' massive denial. But as the months turned into years she finally felt safe enough to share these terrible secrets and healing began. It's been said that "you're only as sick as your secrets" and this was certainly the case for Savannah.

As she gradually came to trust her own memories instead of the whitewashed recollections presented by her parents, Savannah became more and more angry. The sobs became screams of rage as she got in touch with terror, fear, shame, and anger that had been so deeply buried for so many years.

Savannah was able to forgive, but only after she faced the realities of what had actually occurred. Nearly five years after she started treatment, Savannah brought the following composition to therapy for me to read. I think it expresses the extent of her healing better than I can.

Daddy, why did you:

Demand I clean up my life,
while you continued to destroy my life.

Point to God,
While you were selling yourself to the devil.

Demand I be honest,
While you continued to lie.

Watch me cry,
When you knew the tears came from your hands.

Point out my guilt and shame,
only for me to later find out you were causing it.

Show me how to look out for myself,
While convincing me I was helpless against you.

Point the way to self-esteem,
While destroying the path I was to walk on.

Give me seed for my body,
Only to forbid its core to grow.

Show pride and admiration for me by day,
While degrading me at night.

Speak of the power of prayer,
Only to cause me to use it most when you were around.

Encourage me to express myself,
While you numbed my emotions.

Tell me you would protect me from fears,
While causing me the greatest panic.

Well, Daddy, someone has replaced you. Me.

Savannah's forgiveness was deep and broad. As her trust of me grew through the process of psychotherapy, I watched her first **recognize**, then **disconnect**, from the numerous horrors of her past. Flashbacks and nightmares lessened in severity and frequency, and her several personalities gradually integrated into a single cohesive Savannah. She is currently pursuing a successful career as a physical therapist, is happily married to a teacher, and finds the time to mother two children and three cats.

Though Savannah's forgiveness is deep and authentic, it is not the "warm fuzzy" Sunday-school variety we so often promulgate. Nor does it include reconciliation. Unlike the biblical Joseph or the prodigal son, Savannah has no loving father with whom to reconcile. This is a man so thoroughly evil yet so radically self-righteous he would never *ask* to be forgiven. His "apology" would sound more like what has become today's standard political non-apology: "If she misunderstood my intentions, I'm sorry." Or, "I never intended any harm, and if she misread my actions I'm sorry."

Consequently, as therapy progressed, she forgave and "divorced" her parents, gradually coming to see me as a good and safe parent surrogate. For Savannah, psychotherapy was a **corrective emotional experience**, allowing her to develop an intimate relationship with a male who would not exploit her. For her, this was a first.

She now refers to her biological father as her "ex-father." To those unacquainted with the details of Savannah's life, referring to her father as her "ex" may seem unforgiving, but it was only by disconnecting from her family pathology that she could get on with her life; and like a marriage gone awry, referring to her parents as her "exes" allows her to recognize the reality of what once existed, without maintaining a connection. On Father's Day she unfailingly sends me a card with a message of caring from daughter to parent. She always signs "Love, Savannah."

Many clinicians advocate prosecuting the perpetrator, as part of treatment, implying that unless this is done recovery can never be complete. I disagree. Savannah's case illustrates that some victims can recover completely without sending the perpetrator to jail. Although her father deserves to spend the remainder of his life in prison, Savannah does not want to go through complex litigation, be accused by attorneys of "false memory syndrome," and devote several years to prosecuting her biological parent. In her thirties already, she wants to get on with her life and has decided to leave ultimate judgment to God.

Savannah's courageous survival illustrates that some people can **forgive without reconciliation or prosecution**. She has been able to achieve peace without compromising reality. She accepts evil for the horror that it is and leaves ultimate judgment to God. She has forgiven her parents, but because they continue to deny what happened, she is unable to reconcile or to reunite with them. In order to reconcile, she would have to pretend — as they continue to pretend — that nothing wrong ever happened. This would undermine the foundation of truth upon which her recovery progressed.

Kathleen — A Case Study In Self-Forgiveness

She seemed small — almost lost — in the overstuffed leather chair in my office. But as she began anxiously telling her tale, I could easily flip the clock in my mind back thirty years and see a picture-perfect Irish Catholic girl — freckled face, shining green eyes, auburn red hair shining in the sunlight more like copper than freshly scrubbed carrots. She was a "good Catholic girl," regularly attending mass, faithfully bringing home from school not only good grades but commendations from the nuns regarding her exemplary behavior. Throughout her elementary and high school years Kathleen was, by all accounts, perfect.

But one night all this changed. While at the state university she did something for which she had been unable to forgive herself in the subsequent twenty years. She committed the ultimate Catholic twin sins: She engaged in sex before marriage and had an abortion. By the time I saw her, the fresh-scrubbed, squeaky-clean schoolgirl was middle-aged, depressed, and consumed by guilt.

"I have an eating disorder ... always going on diets."

That's how she first described it, but in the months that followed, I learned that it was much more serious than simply going on numerous diets. She engaged in daily binge-and-purge cycles, stuffing herself with up to ten thousand calories at a time and then relieving both her abdomen and conscience by throwing up. This cycle was her darkest secret ... well, almost. Not even her husband knew. I was the first person with whom she shared this secret, and from that moment, healing began.

I'd been seeing Kathleen for nearly two years. Although her progress had been good, she still struggled with what seemed like an "eating disorder," but was in fact an attempt to escape guilt and depression which persistently returned even after weeks or months of freedom from compulsive eating and the subsequent blues.

One day she finally confessed the darkest secret of all, the one that made her feel like a murderer and ultimately caused her to eat and throw up in a futile attempt to assuage her troubled conscience.

"Dr. Berecz, there's something I've never told you."

No words perk up a clinical psychologist's ears more than those. It's like someone screaming, "Fire!" I knew this was going to be,

121

as teens today say, "deep." But now came the sudden halt of words, words drowned by a torrent of tears. Finally, after long minutes of convulsive sobbing, words started slowly, like popcorn, then with machine-gun rat-a-tat-tat: "I ... I ... uh ... well ... ya know ... when ... I ... was at ... the university ... I ... I ... *I-got-an-abortion*!

It was finally out. The *real* secret, the primal tap root of her psychopathology. Finally, after two years of psychotherapy, after twenty-some years of guilt-driven compulsive caring for her husband, compulsive caring for her children, and compulsive eating for herself, Kathleen began the first phase of healing, which was to face her darkest secret. Once this was out, her progress was rapid, and she was able to understand more deeply how her abortion and eating disorder were related:

> *You know, Dr. Berecz, I was thinking about what we talked about last week — you know, what you said about my self-esteem and co-dependency and that stuff. Well, anyway, I did a lot of thinking about it, and I remember two distinct times when I felt totally unworthy. The first was my wedding day. I thought I don't deserve Harold. He's so good, kind, etc., and if he had any idea of what I had done, I'll bet he wouldn't be marrying me. I cried most of the day, and everyone thought it was just because I was nervous, but it was because I felt so guilty.*
>
> *The second time was when my first child was born — without any birth defects — I thought God was going to punish me for the abortion by giving my child birth defects. Actually, I felt that way **each time** I had a child. Even with the fourth one! Isn't that funny? I guess I never got over it really.*
>
> *Well, anyway, it's like we said last week. I think I run around taking care of everybody — Harold, my kids, the people at work, everybody — in order to "make up" for how I really feel inside. Then if that's not enough I have this eating thing as well.*

Recovery for Kathleen occurred when she finally forgave herself for her the abortion, realized she didn't have to "make up" for it the rest of her life, and began to feel more entitled to some self-care. Prior to that, she had cared for everyone else but deeply resented it. Now she is able to balance caring for others with appropriate self-care and has not resorted to using food as a reward for endlessly caring for others. The stress-eat-throw up-guilt cycle has been broken and she travels much more lightly. Less food, less stress, less guilt.

She finally felt worthy enough to attend mass again, and with my encouragement confessed the abortion to her priest. His kindly "Why did you wait so long?" filled her eyes with tears of gratefulness, and he didn't even assign her any penance, saying, "I think you've suffered enough already."

Thus, thrice-forgiven (by herself, her therapist, and her priest) Kathleen was finally free of the terrible guilt that had hung like heavy coils of garden hose round her neck — slowing her steps and stooping her shoulders — much of her early adult life. Now the Irish teenager's sparkle returned to her depressed eyes and she began to play again. Many of her compulsive aerobic workouts (up to two hours each day) were replaced with "fun" sports such as tennis, skiing, swimming, and other activities she actually enjoyed.

Kathleen's personality was primarily healthy, but underneath she had struggled as an obsessive-compulsive. Although she had appeared happy and carefree to others, this had been only a veneer that hid her compulsive need to do everything perfectly.

As she was able to forgive herself, she became less driven to be "perfect" and no longer felt as if she had to do everything flawlessly in order to make up for her hidden badness. And as she left the guilt of her past behind, her stress level came down a couple of notches, leaving her more relaxed and less compulsively "hard working." Her depression lifted, and she found ample energy to pursue life fully.

***

In the subsequent concluding chapter, we will revisit and review much that we've learned about forgiveness, but you may be left with more questions than answers. Perhaps that's as it ought to be, because forgiveness is a complex psychological and spiritual process which, like fingerprints and snowflakes, never occurs twice in precisely the same configuration. When Savannah forgave her parents it was quite a different process from what occurred between the German and English soldiers in that shell-hole of Remarque's *All Quiet on the Western Front.* When Kathleen forgave herself it was again different than anyone else's experience.

Forgiving oneself of numerous past mistakes — reframing them as feedback to guide future behavior — is always uniquely personal. So as we conclude this book, I hope you will develop new insights into your own unique forgiving strategies. And most importantly, I trust such insights will enable you to forgive yourself and others more easily.

Even as I begin to write this final chapter, I know it will leave me less than satisfied. So complex is the human side of forgiveness — leaving excess baggage behind — and so unfathomable the divine side — "While we were yet sinners Christ died for us" — it seems almost presumptuous to try. But try I will, and I hope that you will find insights that will make it easier for you to be generous in forgiving yourself and others.

Yet, on the other hand, it may not be as complicated as we sometimes try to make it. One of my favorite passages of Old Testament scripture elegantly simplifies the formula for the good life:

> *He has showed you, O man, what is good.*
> *And what does the Lord require of you?*
> *To act justly and to love mercy*
> *and to walk humbly with your God.* (Micah 6:8)

You may have already experienced the fulfillment of acting justly and walking humbly with your God, but I hope my final chapter will help you to love mercy a little more.

Finally, I trust that you will grow to understand more clearly the value of disconnecting completely from your own past mistakes and from the pain others may have inflicted upon you. Then you'll be able to forgive yourself and others more thoroughly.

It is humanly impossible to "forgive and *forget*," but as you begin to leave more of your baggage behind, you will likely feel closer to a God who *completely* lets go of our past mistakes:

124

Who is a God like you,
who pardons sin and forgives the transgression ...

You will again have compassion on us;
you will tread our sins underfoot
and hurl all our iniquities into the depths of the sea.
(Micah 7:18, 19)

Chapter 9

Flowers Of Forgiveness

We conclude where we began, with flowers. Forgiving styles, like flowers, show great variation while still retaining unique features. Flowers differ among themselves but share core properties which allow us to recognize a flower as different from a fish or a tree. Forgiveness differs considerably, depending on the style of the person and the features of the situation; but genuine forgiveness always involves **disconnecting from past pain, and re-investing in present purposes and future plans**. These are the blossoms and stems common to all varieties of forgiveness.

Obsessive-compulsives forgive by disconnecting from **details** of past wrongs; histrionics forgive by disconnecting from **feelings** associated with previous wrongs or mistreatments. But whatever the personality style of the forgiver or the attitude of the person requiring forgiveness, all genuine forgiveness involves **disconnecting** from the **past** and living in the **present** and **future**. When you forgive someone you're like the electric company with a delinquent customer. You issue a "disconnect notice" and thereafter shift your energy elsewhere. The "disconnect notice" remains true whether you're forgiving yourself or others.

Forgiving Yourself And Others

Usually it is easier to forgive others than to forgive yourself because in comparing yourself to someone in trouble you often gain status. This is the dynamic that makes gossip so popular. You think, "Look at how much better I am than Elizabeth Jones," as you say, "Did you hear Beth was having an affair with Charlie Smith?" If on top of this ubiquitous "gossip syndrome" (gossipers are morally superior to the persons about whom they gossip) you graciously forgive the people being gossiped about, it makes you doubly better! Not only are they worse than you for cheating on

127

their spouses, you've bettered yourself even more by "forgiving" them for some offense against you.

Even if you don't derive gratification from thinking yourself superior to your "forgivee," it's nonetheless difficult to let go of your own wrongs. The memories of "how I screwed up" are always there in front of your face — easy to access, difficult to forget. No one knows better than you how enraged you became at that salesperson or at the driver who cut you off in traffic. Others heard what you actually said, but you know what you really wanted to say. Others are able to observe your behavior and your actions, but you have access to the deeper layers of your mind and you are intimately acquainted with the corruption that lurks beneath the surface. You know the temptations passed by, the desires gratified only in fantasy, the vituperous words left unspoken. Consequently, when it comes to self, there's more to forgive, more to leave behind.

Forgiving yourself, as Kathleen finally did, means **disconnecting** from the shame, embarrassment, ridicule, and humiliation of previous failures and mistakes. It means living in the light of present potentialities rather than the shadow of past pain. It involves realizing that one cannot "make up" for past failures or mistakes by planning to be perfect in the future. Far better to **reframe** past mistakes as **feedback** — useful in guiding future behavior — than to attempt errorless living. Such attempts are certain to fail, generating more shame and diminishing self-esteem even further.

Forgiving others means **disconnecting** from fantasies of retaliation and revenge and channeling the energy of anger into new projects with new people. An unforgiving Savannah might have spent her entire life as a career victim. Even after therapy, she could have chronically carried some anger, hate, and resentment, possibly even channeling this into a career of helping other abused victims. Instead, through the healing of forgiveness, she is pursuing a completely new life — a life to which her "exes" have no access. They weren't invited to her wedding. She doesn't return their phone calls. They'll never see their grandchildren. This isn't because Savannah is holding a "grudge" but because they refuse to repent, to admit what happened, and to seek forgiveness. Consequently, forgiving them cannot include reconciliation because Savannah would have to pretend that nothing had ever happened, and she knows this is untrue.

What Forgiveness Is Not

I'd like to conclude this book by consolidating the key characteristics of forgiveness. But before doing that I'll briefly discuss what forgiveness is not, because like all genuine products forgiveness has numerous counterfeits.

Forgiveness is not enmeshment. Too often dependency is mistaken for love, and enmeshment counterfeits as forgiveness. Enmeshing parents, such as Savannah's parents, create enmeshed families where "my business is my business, and your business is my business." In families without boundaries children fail to develop adequate self-direction, because moves in the direction of individuality and uniqueness are squelched by parents who may be too insecure to allow their children to differ from them, or who may have hidden motives to exploit their children.

Forgiveness in such a family requires *not* reunion — there's already too much "closeness" — but rather separation and individuation. Here "letting go" takes priority over "getting together." Forgiveness *without* reconciliation may seem half-baked to those who have grown up hearing forgiveness plus reconciliation stories, but healthy forgiveness often necessitates deleting the romantic "and-they-lived-happily-after" endings.

Forgiveness is not necessarily reconciliation. Forgiving *may* include reconciliation, reunion, or harmony, as in the Old Testament story of Joseph forgiving his brothers, or the New Testament parable of the prodigal son returning home. However, as Savannah's story vividly illustrates, you may authentically forgive without liking the person you're forgiving. This is important, because if we make forgiveness into a "warm fuzzy" we will be imprisoned by that notion. If, instead, we understand how to **disconnect** and move on with our lives, we will be free to forgive even our enemies. Sometimes this will occur when we see them as siblings and actually begin to like them, but often this will not be the case.

No doubt we ought to try achieving reconciliation whenever possible, since this will spread the healing balm of forgiveness across the wounds on both sides of broken relationships. When forgiveness is accompanied by reconciliation, it increases the likelihood that the forgiveness will remain dynamic and active and continue to heal. Much as members of Alcoholics Anonymous solidify their commitment to sobriety by actively helping others to stop drinking, people who forgive *and* reconcile have a better chance of maintaining their gains. However, as we've seen in Savannah's case, reconciliation is not always possible, and forgiveness can occur without it.

Forgiveness is not fairness. This is particularly difficult for some people to accept, especially if they are obsessive. Such people long to live in a world that is orderly, punctual, clean, safe, and *fair*. But such a world is an illusion. Nowhere — not even in scripture — is it suggested that fairness is obtainable on this planet. Forgiveness sometimes includes what seems to all parties a "fair" settlement, but this is not an essential ingredient. Expecting fairness strangles the life out of forgiveness, because a "just" and even-handed settlement is seldom achieved.

This is especially obvious in cases like Savannah's where children or weaker people are abused by others more powerful. It wasn't fair that Savannah's father misused her, but she was nonetheless able to disconnect and move on with her life. This getting on with your life and allowing the forgiven to get on with theirs is the essential core of forgiveness, not whether you got a "square deal."

One of the essentials of a forgiving attitude is a recognition that unfairness is an integral part of reality. This truth seldom comes as a sudden epiphany; it occurs typically in a piecemeal fashion — gradually and with difficulty. This was well illustrated in a personal experience shared on NPR's *Morning Edition*, broadcast on March 4, 1992. The commentator, Mary Ann Watson, told the following story:

> *The second graders at Our Lady Queen of Apostles school stood in line waiting to pick slips of paper out of a fishbowl sitting on Sister's desk in front of the classroom. Whatever was written on the paper that we pulled was what we had to give up for Lent.*

It was a somber occasion. No giggling or pushing. We were serious seven-year-olds all set to sacrifice.

As each child drew from the fishbowl he or she would read aloud what would be abstained for the forty days until Palm Sunday, plus the six days of Holy Week — an amount of time just short of eternity.

The first slip drawn was "Soda Pop." The boy standing behind me about mid-way through the line was the only child brazen enough to react. "Oh man," he blurted out, "that's rough."

One by one the children announced their offerings. "Comic Books." "Ice cream." "Chocolate." "Movies." "Potato Chips." "Cakes and pies." Candy bars." "Cookies."

Then it was my turn. I reached way down to the bottom — the way they did when they picked the door prize at Bingo. I opened the slip and couldn't believe my eyes. I was too stunned to speak for an instant. There were just two letters on the paper — TV. It might as well have said oxygen.

When I was finally able to inform my waiting class-mates that I would give up television for Lent there was a collective gasp. Looks of pity came from the children who had already had their turn and looks of horror came from those still waiting in line wondering if there were any duplicates in the fishbowl.

I was still numb when the boy behind me picked up his slip. A big smile came across his face and he read "Pret-zels." "Wait a minute," I thought. "I give up TV, and he gives up pretzels and we're even?!" I truly wanted to be in a state of grace, but this was martyrdom plain and simple.

*I struggled with my fate that Lent. A few times the temp-tation to sneak a peek at the screen was just too great. But mostly I accepted my burden. And on Easter Sunday morning, after Mass, I watched **Davey and Goliath** a changed person.*

At the tender age of seven I learned that a lot of life is the luck of the draw. Though it was devastating at the time, I'm grateful that my introduction to the horror of randomness was so benign.

It's one thing, of course, to be precocious about the vicissitudes of life. It's a bit more of a developmental achievement not to begrudge the indiscriminate good luck of someone else standing in line at the same fishbowl.
I'm still working on it.

Forgiveness is not appeasement or submission. This distinction is particularly crucial when discussing forgiveness in the case of persons we call co-dependent. As previously noted, all that glitters is not gold. Co-dependent "forgiveness" is all too often a cover for appeasement or submission. What looks like forgiveness is frequently psychological fawning. Such pacification does not allow you to disconnect and get on with your life, because you'll often be drawn right back into the circle of destructiveness, as we've already seen in spouse-abuse cycles. It is doubly damaging in reinforcing the pathology of the perpetrator, and in providing a veneer that protects the co-dependent from dealing with his or her own underlying psychological insecurities. It takes strength for the co-dependent *not* to reconcile with the abuser.

This is well illustrated in J. Smiley's recent novel *A Thousand Acres*. In one of the final scenes, two sisters — both of whom have been sexually abused by their father — are at the hospital where one of them is dying of cancer:

> *I stood up. "I should go. I promised them."*
> *She reached for my hand. Hers was cool, and her thumbnail dug into my palm. She jerked me toward her. She said, "I have no accomplishments. I didn't teach long enough to know what I was doing. I didn't make a good life with Pete. I didn't shepherd my daughters into adulthood. I didn't win Jess Clark. I didn't work the farm successfully. I was as much of a nothing as Mommy or Grandma Edith. I didn't even get Daddy to know what he had done, or what it meant. People around town talk about how I wrecked it all. Three generations on the same farm, great land, Daddy a marvelous farmer, and a saint to boot." She used my hand to pull herself up in bed. "So all I have is the knowledge that I saw! That I saw without being afraid and without turning away, and that I didn't*

forgive the unforgivable. Forgiveness is a reflex for when
you can't stand what you know. I resisted that reflex. That's
my sole, solitary, lonely accomplishment."
   I extricated my hand.
Rose closed her eyes and waved me out the door. (p. 384)

Co-dependent believers typically see God as a divine co-dependent, limitlessly forgiving all sins, and this is comforting to them because they rationalize they are "divinely" forgiving others. The big difference, however, is that while God forgives from a position of strength, co-dependents forgive out of insecurity. To use Rose's words, they "forgive the unforgivable."

Forgiveness is not necessarily pardon. Pardon means to excuse an offense without penalty. The emphasis is on remission of penalty, release from punishment. **Forgive,** on the other hand, is defined by Webster as: 1) To cease to feel resentment against (an offender); 2 a) to give up resentment of or claim to requital for an insult; b) to grant relief from payment of a debt.

Notice that although granting relief from payment of a debt is mentioned, the primary emphasis is on *letting go of resentment.* Certainly there will be times when forgiveness also includes pardon — bypassing punishment — but this is not necessary at all times. Parents, for example, ought to be *forgiving* (not harboring resentment) towards their children, but not *pardoning* (bypassing consequences). One could forgive a child for messing up the living room *and* require him to clean up the clutter.

Forgiveness can be lonely. Although I didn't discuss the details of her therapy, I must mention that Savannah's biggest struggle was in letting go of her family. She experienced tremendous loneliness in the process of disconnecting from her family. In addition to losing her parents, she also had to give up her siblings, all of whom "knew" Dad could never have done anything so horrible. Forgiveness without reconciliation may be necessary, but it is nevertheless lonely, and leaving your excess luggage at the airport requires a lot of courage.

Forgiveness can be confusing. In addition to missing her siblings, Savannah sometimes even missed Daddy! Like many victims of childhood sexual abuse she was left with confusingly mixed feelings. In the beginning the "night games" had terrorized her, but since her father was skilled in sexual stimulation and since he had access to drugs as well, he was able to create an experience that was *biologically* pleasurable while at the same time *psychologically* devastating. Letting go of Daddy wasn't easy.

When forgiveness involves *letting go* (without reconciliation), it is akin to grief work, and mourning is seldom "warm and fuzzy." It hurts, it's painful, it takes time, and it's *not* fun. When you let go of a long-term "friend" or acquaintance — even one that hurt you — you're going to be lonely for a while. It takes time to fill the empty spaces with new friends. Savannah had to find an entire new family, and often she wasn't sure she wanted to. She sometimes picked up the phone and called home even though it would upset her for days afterward.

The Nature Of Forgiveness

Sometimes we find it difficult to put forgiveness in practical terms, because in scripture forgiveness is often illustrated with legal, financial, or political stories. A king treats someone who owes him a large debt kindly; a master deals gently with a runaway slave; a wealthy landowner "forgives" a debt.

But today few of us employ servants other than those who help us with child care or occasional cleaning, and if we can afford to buy some help with housecleaning or landscaping, we're likely to treat our employees more as equals than indentured servants. Biblical illustrations of forgiveness in terms of kings and servants, masters and slaves, leave most of us feeling distant from the process.

Consequently in this book I've tried to take forgiveness "out of church" and return it to the workplace, where people rudely jostle one another for the opportunity to be first in line at a Bloomingdale's sale, or become irate over a waitress' error in ordering the steak medium/rare instead of rare. I'll begin with a basic axiom:

Forgiving is a process. It's a process — like learning to play the piano — that occurs gradually over time, and the cliche which advises us to "forgive and forget" is psychological nonsense. In this respect forgiving is much like grieving, a stepwise process that takes time and includes "unacceptable" emotions such as anger, resentment, depression, and despair. The process of trying to

134

put trauma out of mind often prolongs the healing process because people avoid dealing with the real issues. We simply cannot "slam the door" on the past; when we've been abandoned or psychologically hurt, such injuries often become **internalized** as **shame**.

Shame destroys self-esteem from the inside. It is a **contemporary conglomerate** of *past* ridicule, experienced as a seeping sense of badness, permeating the self with a toxic tide of censure. Most of us remember being teased. Those searing moments in which we were the target of ridicule are not easily forgotten. However, as adults, even though we experience little direct teasing, shame can be reactivated by a variety of encounters far removed from the original ridicule.

It isn't my purpose to discuss shame thoroughly; rather, in the present context, I want to emphasize that genuinely forgiving someone who hurts you in the present is complex enough. Forgiving past abuse, teasing, and torment is extremely difficult because it has long since been internalized as part of the self-concept, and now reoccurs in the form of shame.

Here is where our study of how to love yourself becomes relevant. Forgiving hurts of the past — getting rid of the contemporary shame conglomerates — is a process that requires what psychoanalysts term "working through." It means that over and over, time after time, in one new situation after another, you confront the old ghosts, until gradually they leave you alone.

Forgiving is more like going round and round in a revolving door than walking through a conventional door and locking it shut. You get into anger, self-pity, shame, or a variety of negative emotions which often occur when you fail to disconnect from a hurtful incident. You alternate between feelings of fury or forgiveness. Back and forth, over and over; but finally, more and more slowly. Finally, much like a revolving door coming to rest, you're able to go in one side, come out the other, and walk away. But this takes time, and no one but you knows when the work is complete. Like grieving and other healing processes, forgiving defies precise timetables. This is not a once-and-for-all event; it is a go-at-your-own-pace process, so set your own pace. Good luck!

If you're "lucky" forgiveness becomes easier. Luck is a bit like table salt. It enhances the flavor of life and makes forgiving easier. We've seen how our tendency to blame others is directly related to how many degrees of freedom we assign to them in choosing their behavior. We've noted that such degrees of freedom are usually divided between the person and the situation, that the more responsibility we assign to the environment, the less likely we are to blame the person. But even so, we're always trying to partition blame — to the person, to the situation, even to God.

But in forgiving ourselves, others, and God we seldom assign enough importance to the role of luck. We've already discussed this in Chapter 2, but we need to remind ourselves of luck often, because we're prone to hold others and ourselves too responsible, thus making it more difficult to forgive.

If, for example, we really view tornados, floods, earthquakes, or other disasters in insurance-company terms, "acts of God," we'll find the tragedies even more sinister than they are. The problem with many believers is that they believe in a very interventionist God, and are then left with a subconsciously *blaming* attitude when bad things happen. An interventionist God is a blameworthy God.

Forgiving God is necessary for some people. I recently attended a symposium on forgiveness where someone in the audience, during the question-and-answer period following the presentation, asked, "What about forgiving God? How can we learn to forgive God?" To some in the audience the question seemed stunning — sacreligious. How could we humans — mere specks of cosmic dust — pretend to forgive the Almighty? What arrogance to discuss such nonsense! The panel members adroitly sidestepped the question, saying it was a "matter of theology" how one dealt with forgiving God.

I think this has more to do with psychological style than theology. Obsessive-compulsive people like to believe that the universe is an orderly place where somebody (God, for one) is in **control**. Random evil, bad luck, or chance misfortunes are frightening to the obsessive. Much preferred is the illusion that *everything* is under control.

Recently in my community a nine-year-old boy died of injuries he suffered when a heavy mound of sand and clay collapsed on him and his eleven-year-old brother as they played on the beach near their home. Local authorities said a large chunk of an approximately fifty-foot-high bluff gave way and fell on the boys. Our local paper reported that his parents stressed that they didn't feel they were in any way negligent in their son's death:

"It was an act of God," the parents said. "We know he was saved. We know God took him home."

The paper reported that the stretch of shoreline had been eroding recently at a fast pace, and that Zachary's parents, who had lived in their home for about a year, said they had no idea of the danger their children were in.

To such people — those who believe that a sandy bluff collapsing on a child is simply God's way of "taking him home" — forgiving God might be unnecessary. I think needing to forgive God is most common among the obsessive personality styles.

Ever notice how badly you want to believe you're in control of things after you've had a minor accident? Remember the last time you had a "fender bender"? Some variant of the following thoughts probably crossed your mind: "Shoot! If only I had left five minutes earlier, this wouldn't have happened!" Or, "Doggone! I knew I should have taken the other route! I've never liked this intersection!" Or, "I should have taken the car in and gotten snow tires as I was planning to! Then this wouldn't have happened!"

Such self-blaming thoughts regularly occur to all of us in times of difficulty. Why do we scan our minds for "explanations" with which to punish ourselves? Because we would rather punish ourselves than to believe that the world is not predictable. We would rather place ourselves in the center of causality than to think we're subject to random happenings. It's frightening to believe that as I drive to work, I might just happen to hit a slippery spot on the road and have the bad luck to do so while approaching an eighteen-wheeler. Better to believe that I'm in control — even if I have to do it by *retroactively musing* about the many ways I could have prevented this accident.

I believe the universe is generally under God's surveillance (read *control*, if you're obsessive), and things happen within His broadly based boundaries. However, specific events may occur somewhat randomly. This makes it easier for me to "forgive" God and others when bad things happen. By this I don't mean to sound blasphemous and suggest that *I* forgive the Almighty in any moral sense, but rather I can let go of my bitterness towards Him, just as I can let go of it towards other people.

I think of God as a great golfer: He plays the course with the game well under control, but the ball still takes bad bounces as well as some lucky bounces occasionally. The outcome of the game is never in doubt — He will win, at well under par — but precisely where the ball lands after being struck is always influenced by how the ball was hit, and the luck of the bounce.

Forgiving means good-enough living. As we noted in Chapter 6, while other professionals were pointing out the many ways in which mothers fail, the English psychoanalyst Winnicott introduced the refreshing concept of "good-enough" mothering (1975).

Winnicott's notion of *good enough* is particularly apropos to our understanding of forgiveness. Recall it was the morally meticulous Pharisees — not Christ — who hounded their hapless listeners to strive to become more flawless.

"But," you might ask, "wasn't it Jesus who said, 'Be perfect, therefore, as your heavenly Father is perfect' (Matthew 5:48)?"

Indeed, these were the words of Jesus, but they were not a call to perfectionism or moral scrupulosity. The original Greek word that was translated "perfect" really means completeness or wholeness. It does not mean error free or flawless. We're encouraged to be wholesome and complete (here on earth, in our sphere) *as the Father in heaven*. This suggests two different arenas of operation ("on earth as it is in heaven"), *not* a striving for divine perfection.

We've seen that forgiving is sometimes a lonely process which involves disconnecting from past mistakes and hurts. It involves letting go of control and even assigning some happenings to luck. Finally, it means freedom from obsessive perfectionism. But I can imagine you saying, "That all sounds fine, but how can I bring it about?" A fair question. Psychologically speaking, **forgiving means reframing**.

Forgiving Is Reframing

Forgiving by reframing is one of the most crucial psychological insights I can share with you. As you begin to comprehend how reframing offers an authentic way out of "no-win" confrontations, you'll find it easier to forgive.

In simplest terms, reframing means to **see something in a new light**. Tom Sawyer reframed punishment as play in the famous incident that began when Aunt Polly caught him sneaking in a window late one night and decided to turn his Saturday holiday into "hard labor" by requiring him to whitewash the fence (Twain, 1982). We now join Tom:

> Tom appeared on the sidewalk with a bucket of white-wash and a long-handled brush. He surveyed the fence, and all gladness left him and a deep melancholy settled down upon his spirit. Thirty yards of board fence, nine feet high. Life to him seemed hollow, and existence but a burden.... (p. 10)

When Jim, one of Tom's friends, came skipping along on his way to get water from the town pump, Tom eagerly offered to trade jobs:

> "Say, Jim, I'll fetch the water if you'll whitewash some."
> Jim shook his head and said: "Can't, Mars Tom. Ole missis, she tole me I got to go an' git dis water an' not stop foolin' roun' wid anybody. She say she spec' Mars Tom gwyne to ax me to whitewash, an' she tole me 'long an' 'tend to my own business." (p. 11)

So as his energy began to lag and he thought of all the fun he'd planned for this day, all the excitement his friends would be having, Tom changed tactics, successfully reframing during his next encounter:

> He took up his brush and went tranquilly to work. Ben Rogers hove in sight presently — the very boy, of all boys, whose ridicule he had been dreading. Ben's gait was the

hop-skip-and-jump — *proof enough that his heart was light and his anticipations high ... Ben stared a moment and then said: "Hi-yi!* **You're** *up a stump, ain't you!"*

No answer. Tom surveyed his last touch with the eye of an artist; then he gave his brush another gentle sweep and surveyed the result, as before. Ben ranged up alongside of him. Tom's mouth watered for the apple, but he stuck to his work. Ben said: "Hello, old chap, you got to work hey?"

Tom wheeled suddenly and said: "Why it's you, Ben! I warn't noticing."

"Say — I'm going in a-swimming, I am. Don't you wish you could? But of course you'd druther work — wouldn't you? 'Course you would!"

Tom contemplated the boy a bit, and said: "What do you call work?"

"Why ain't **that** *work?"*

Tom resumed his whitewashing, and answered carelessly: "Well, maybe it is, and maybe it ain't. All I know is, it suits Tom Sawyer."

"Oh come, now, you don't mean to let on that you **like** *it?"*

The brush continued to move. "Like it? Well I don't see why I oughtn't to like it. Does a boy get a chance to whitewash a fence every day?"

That put the thing in a new light. Ben stopped nibbling his apple. Tom swept his brush daintily back and forth — stepped back to note the effect — added a touch here and there — criticised the effect again — Ben watching every move and getting more and more interested, more and more absorbed. Presently he said: "Say, Tom, let me whitewash a little." (pp. 12-14)

Tom gave up the brush with reluctance in his face but alacrity in his heart. And while [Ben] worked and sweated in the sun, the retired artist sat on a barrel in the shade close by, dangled his legs, munched his apple, and planned the slaughter of more innocents. There was no lack of material; boys happened along every little while; they came to jeer, but remained to whitewash. By the time Ben was fagged out, Tom had traded the next chance to Billy

Fisher for a kite, in good repair; and when he played out, Johnny Miller bought in for a dead rat and a string to swing it with — and so on, and so on, hour after hour. And when the middle of the afternoon came, from being a poor poverty-stricken boy in the morning, Tom was literally rolling in wealth. He had, beside the things before mentioned, twelve marbles, part of a jews-harp, a piece of blue bottle-glass to look through, a spool cannon, a key that wouldn't unlock anything, a fragment of chalk, a glass stopper of a decanter, a tin soldier, a couple of tadpoles, six fire-crackers, a kitten with only one eye, a brass doorknob, a dog collar — but no dog — the handle of a knife, four pieces of orange peel, and a dilapidated old window sash.

He had had a nice, good, idle time all the while — plenty of company — and the fence had three coats of whitewash on it! If he hadn't run out of whitewash, he would have bankrupted every boy in the village. (p. 15)

Mark Twain's timeless Tom Sawyer here illustrates **reframing** as a process allowing him creatively to **escape** the confines of Aunt Polly's penalty. Tom transforms work into play — punishment into profit. Reframing allows us to escape the confines of dichotomous dilemmas by creatively escaping to **higher-order solutions**. Without reframing we become mired in the illusion that we must choose **one** of **only two** possible alternatives. Like a hapless witness in the courtroom wishing to "explain" — speak more broadly — we are confined by the prosecuting attorney's "Yes or no?" and the judge's admonition, "Just answer the question."

We are easily trapped by the apparent dichotomies which surround us — work and play, right and wrong, good and evil — too often failing to find the higher-order solution by reframing. Forgiveness is the quintessential reframer not only of moral dilemmas, but of life itself. Jesus Christ, the "Tom Sawyer" of the New Testament, constantly escaped the dichotomous moral traps of the scribes and Pharisees by reframing.

In the most famous of New Testament forgiveness stories, the dignified professor, Jesus Christ, teaching in the temple, reframes the lawyers and Pharisees by suddenly interrupting His verbal lecture and stooping to write words in the sand:

> *At dawn he [Jesus] appeared again in the temple courts, where all the people gathered around him, and he sat down to teach them. The teachers of the law and the Pharisees brought in a woman caught in adultery. They made her stand before the group and said to Jesus, "Teacher, this woman was caught in the act of adultery. In the Law Moses commanded us to stone such women. Now what do you say?" They were using this question as a trap, in order to have a basis for accusing him.*
>
> *But Jesus bent down and started to write on the ground with his finger. When they kept on questioning him, he straightened up and said to them, "If any one of you is without sin, let him be the first to throw a stone at her." Again he stooped down and wrote on the ground.*
>
> *At this, those who heard began to go away one at a time, the older ones first, until only Jesus was left, with the woman still standing there. Jesus straightened up and asked her, "Woman, where are they? Has no one condemned you?"*
>
> *"No one, sir," she said.*
>
> *"Then neither do I condemn you," Jesus declared. "Go now and leave your life of sin."* (John 8:2-11)

Even more profound than the great teacher's reframing from verbal communication to the silence of the sands was His reframing of their binary moral trap, "Is she guilty *or* innocent? — Shall we stone her *or* (implied) ignore the Law of Moses?" Jesus escaped to the next higher level and reframed the dilemma as a moral synthesis: No one is perfect. Who is prepared to accuse anyone?

Although the Scriptures are not specific, many believe that Jesus was writing the individual sins of the accusers in the sand, and as they became aware of what was happening, they began to slink away, one by one. The essential point is that Jesus dramatically reframed the Pharisees by changing communication channels — speech to sand — and by exposing the accusers' own sins. In this

142

way he broke out of their binary snares and moved to the higher question of who is qualified to adjudicate the guilt or innocence of another, finally declaring that He, Himself, would not judge.

Most of Jesus' teachings can be seen as reframes of the moral dichotomies which imprisoned the people of His time. The pinnacle of moral reframing is found in the Sermon on the Mount (Matthew 5-8) where, after pronouncing blessings on the marginalized of His society (the poor and the persecuted, the meek and the hungry), He reframes the moral "sacred cows," synthesizing them into higher-level discussions.

Judicial debates about how to treat murderers and adulteresses are reframed as dynamic discussions about anger and lust. The simple sentencing guidelines "eye for an eye, and tooth for a tooth" are reframed into a creative discussion about cheerfully giving up not only your tunic but also your cloak in a lawsuit; of volunteering to tote your oppressor's baggage twice the required distance; of praying for those who persecute you. The two favorite pastimes of the scribes and Pharisees, prayer and fasting, are reframed as inconsequential when compared to giving to the needy.

Such reframes incurred the wrath of the clergy and politicians, but won Him the admiration of the ordinary: "When Jesus had finished saying these things, the crowds were amazed at his teaching, because he taught as one who had authority, and not as their teachers of the law" (Matthew 7:28-29).

Perhaps this is why the eminent sociologist Hannah Arendt wrote:

> *The discoverer of the role of forgiveness in the realm of human affairs was Jesus of Nazareth. The fact that he made this discovery in a religious context and articulated it in religious language is no reason to take it any less seriously in a strictly secular sense.* (1958, p. 238)

Arendt emphasizes forgiveness as crucial to human action because it allows us to escape from the permanence of past behaviors, from what she terms the "predicament of irreversibility."

Without being forgiven, released from the consequences of what we have done, our capacity to act would, as it were, be confined to one single deed from which we could never recover. We would remain the victims of its consequences forever, not unlike the sorcerer's apprentice who lacked the magic formula to break the spell. (1958, p. 237)

And "break the spell" He did! Jesus reframed with agility, leaving behind past mistakes and dead-end dichotomies and shifting to the higher considerations of present potentialities and future promise. His reframes were open-ended and creative, escaping the cognitive conundrums of the Pharisees and providing His listeners unlimited opportunities to evolve, as in the following exchange:

Hearing that Jesus had silenced the Sadducees, the Pharisees got together. One of them, an expert in the law, tested him with this question: "Teacher, which is the greatest commandment in the Law?"

Jesus replied: " 'Love the Lord your God with all your soul and with all your mind.' This is the first and greatest commandment. And the second is like it: 'Love your neighbor as yourself.' All the Law and the Prophets hang on these two commandments." (Matthew 22:34-40)

Notice, Jesus reframes the complexities of their *entire* legal and theological structures into simply loving God, self, and others. This now opens new and interesting questions such as "Who is my neighbor?" which Jesus creatively reframes with a parable:

"A man was going down from Jerusalem to Jericho, when he fell into the hands of robbers. They stripped him of his clothes, beat him and went away, leaving him half dead. A priest happened to be going down the same road, and when he saw the man, he passed by on the other side. So too, a Levite, when he came to the place and saw him, passed by on the other side. But a Samaritan, as he traveled, came where the man was; and when he saw him, he took pity on him. He went to him and bandaged his

wounds, pouring on oil and wine. Then he put the man on his own donkey, took him to an inn and took care of him. The next day he took out two silver coins and gave them to the innkeeper. 'Look after him,' he said 'and when I return, I will reimburse you for any extra expense you may have.'

Which of these three do you think was a neighbor to the man who fell into the hands of robbers?"

The expert in the law replied, "The one who had mercy on him."

Jesus told him, "Go and do likewise." (Luke 10:30-37)

Not only did the parable point out the hypocrisy of the establishment — priest and Levite pass by — it cut to the core of Jewish nationalism, racism, and other boundaries of exclusiveness which divide God's children into "us-or-them" camps. In reply to Jesus, the lawyer was so prejudiced that he couldn't even utter the "S word." Instead of saying "Samaritan" he substituted "the one who had mercy on him."

Reframing means **seeing things in a new light — moving to a higher level of analysis**. Commenting on this parable, Thielicke notes that the priest who "passed by on the other side" consciously tried to avoid *seeing the victim in a new light*:

> *So the priest passed on the other side. This is a sign that this pacification of his conscience did not work quite smoothly after all. He made a wide detour around the poor man in order not to see him. For the sight of him might accuse him and take away from him all his good reasons ...*
>
> *None of us really wants to see. For to look at our neighbor's misery is the first step in brotherly love. Love always seizes the eyes first and then the hand. If I close my eyes, my hands remain unemployed. And finally my conscience too falls asleep, for this disquieting neighbor has disappeared from my sight. Therefore at the Last Judgment it is our eyes that will be judged first. When Jesus says to the people at the Last Judgment, "It was I whom you met in the naked, the hungry, the imprisoned, and*

*you did not help me," it is highly characteristic that the accused should reply, "Lord, when did we **see** thee hungry or thirsty or naked or sick?"* (Matthew 25:44). (1959, p. 166)

I've tried to show how Jesus reframed dichotomous debates into expansive new perceptions which included even hated social outsiders as neighbors. But He didn't even stop there; He ultimately challenged His listeners actively to thrust themselves into life. The lawyer comes seeking intellectualized debate and leaves with the challenge "Go and do likewise" ringing in his ears. Jesus reframes jaded judicial jargon into marketplace mercy. Thielicke puts it well:

*But we cannot go and do and love, if we stop and ask first, "Who is my neighbor?" The devil has been waiting for us to ask this question; and he will always whisper into our ears only the most convenient answers. No, we can love only if we have the mind of Jesus and turn the lawyer's question around. Then we shall not ask "Who is my neighbor?" but "To whom am **I** a neighbor? Who is laid at **my** door? Who is expecting help from **me** and who looks upon **me** as his neighbor?" This reversal of the question is precisely the point of the parable.* (Thielicke, 1959, p. 168)

In summary, reframing is the very heart of forgiving, allowing us to **disconnect** from the past and creatively move into the present and future. We've seen how skillfully reframing was used by Tom Sawyer and Jesus. I hope you'll be able to make it part of your life as well, so please "forgive" one more analogy.

Reframing is like shifting gears. When I first learned to drive, I sometimes became so engrossed in steering, watching the road, and keeping an eye on the rear-view mirror that I would forget to shift to a higher gear, until the whining of the over-revving engine would cause my instructor to shout above the din, "Shift!" When I did, we entered a new realm. The engine calmed down, we moved along more easily, and we covered more distance.

146

Some of you might find this analogy remote, because unlike me, who learned to drive three-speed cars and ride one-speed bikes, you learned to drive one-speed "automatic" cars and eighteen-speed bikes. But whether we ride eighteen-speed bikes, or drive four-by-four ATVs, shifting gears still remains important, because shifting — whether up or down — solves energy problems by qualitatively changing things. When you're running out of power, it doesn't really help to push harder on the gas pedal or on your bicycle pedals. That might temporarily help a bit, but you will be limited by the range of that particular gear, and "giving it more gas" or "pumping harder" won't help much. You have to *shift* to a different level; *change* your paradigm; *switch* perspectives; *see* things in a new light.

Jake

He was both depressed and anxious when I first saw him. Handsomely attired in pinstriped suit and contrasting primary color tie, he worked as vice president for marketing at a large corporation. His late-thirtyish face had far too many wrinkles, especially above and between his eyebrows. He didn't look content and the tension was palpable.

Jake had grown up with alcoholic parents. When he was a boy his parents both lived in perpetual states of intoxication while still seeming to function. His father, who worked in a body shop, literally drank a case of beer each day. Jake could hardly recall seeing his father without a can of beer in his hand or nearby. "Maybe when he showered he didn't have one — although I wouldn't absolutely bet on it."

Mom, though not as obviously alcoholic, was nonetheless emotionally unavailable — depressed, asleep, dozing, resting, napping, she was never around when he needed her. In therapy Jake realized for the first time that Mom's many "naps" were states of intoxication.

As an adult Jake was a compulsive pleaser, co-dependently trying to care for everyone instead of himself. Consequently, he found it almost impossible to express anger. Outwardly, he appeared meek, long-suffering, and gentle, but inwardly he was seething with long-repressed anger. However, since others only observed his excessively compliant outward behavior, they tended to take advantage of him and this further increased Jake's fury.

Although at work he was the "boss," it seemed he was always doing extra things for others like staying late or working weekends to cover for others on vacation. He was experiencing marriage problems because he did so much at home, but didn't feel appreciated. Even sexually, he was always the "orgasm giver" but seldom felt his wife attended to his emotional needs.

In psychotherapy, Jake learned to express anger, become less co-dependently compliant, and mourn the loss of a childhood he never experienced. He became more honest in expressing his needs at home and his marriage improved significantly. But he still found it difficult to forgive his parents for robbing him of his childhood through their alcoholism. Although both had joined AA and been sober for over a decade, this didn't assuage Jake's bitterness.

In therapy I didn't encourage Jake to "pretend" liking his parents or to force "niceness" when he didn't feel it, since this was the very problem that had brought him into treatment in the first place. We had been fairly successful in breaking the cycle of compulsive niceness followed by resentment, but his relationship with his parents remained distant. Then came a breakthrough that sometimes rewards patient psychotherapists. And it wasn't even my doing!

"Little Jake" (they called him "JJ" for John Jacob, Jr.) was born. With the birth of this baby, Jake saw a side of his parents he didn't know existed. Since they were now sober, they responded with rich emotions to their first grandchild. Sometimes this kind of behavior by previously-negligent parents-turned-grandparents causes resentment in their children, who ask, "Why weren't you ever there for me?" But this was not the case for Jake. As he saw his parents tenderly love his new son, it created a bond of closeness Jake had never experienced before. In terms of our current discussion, it allowed Jake to reframe his parents. Instead of negligent, intoxicated alcoholics, he came to see them as the loving people they had become without alcohol in their lives.

And that's how forgiving works in everyday life. By shifting gears you can sometimes see yourself and others in a new light.

Empowered by divine forgiveness, which bestows on you membership in God's family, you can see yourself and others as *His* children. By releasing you from the drag of your own mistakes and from obsessions about how others have hurt you, forgiveness provides you with energy to function creatively in the present and power to spare for the future. And sometimes unplanned things occur — like the birth of JJ — which reframe old relationships in healing new ways.

The Cybernetics Of Forgiveness

Ashby (1961) defined cybernetics as "the art of **steermanship**." Two key concepts in cybernetics are **black boxes** and **feedback**. In social human interactions **forgiveness is a "black box," providing feedback in cybernetic systems**.

Engineers use the term **black box** for a device that contains unknown components. It accepts signals and **transforms** them. By varying the input and observing the output, we can conclude certain things about the nature of the box's components without completely understanding them. Thus, although our knowledge of the human brain is still fragmentary, we nonetheless proceed to analyze how it functions in the system. Most body systems are only understood in black-box kinds of ways.

Blood, for example, at any given moment is a kind of feedback system on the state of the body. By sampling blood and measuring various components we can ascertain many things about the condition of the system without completely analyzing each biochemical component of blood. Thus blood functions as a "black box" of the body, providing feedback.

Forgiveness is like a black box in a cybernetic system. You don't have to understand it completely in order to appropriate its benefits. Forgiveness has the ability to transform negative inputs such as mistakes and mistreatment into positive outcomes, which then provide feedback about how life works.

Forgiving enables you to reframe mistakes and mistreatment as feedback. This is both freeing and energizing, because it allows you to use your own errors and the insults of others to fine-tune your behavior. Striving for errorless living or expecting undeviating kindness from others are seen as obsessive-compulsive illusions. Like major league ballplayers we reframe (forgive) our failures by realizing that getting on base once every three times is "excellent" and not worrying as much about the approximately-two-out-of-three times we "fail."

Trial-and-error is not a symptom of sloppy living, but rather the very **essence** of our humanity. Rather than allowing ourselves to become mired in our own mistakes, or permanently victimized by others, forgiveness energizes us to live fully. This makes good sense psychologically, theologically, and even cybernetically!

In cybernetics, **feedback** is defined as **the return to input of part of the output** of a machine, system, or process. For engineers there are two different kinds of feedback (negative and positive), and Ashby uses the example of a child's train — the kind that runs along a floor, not tracks — to illustrate feedback. If the cars are slightly out of line, trying to back them up (negative feedback) only worsens the problem, but *pulling* them with the engine (positive feedback) straightens the cars. This is why semi-trailers are pulled, not pushed, down the highway by their drivers.

Applying the notion of feedback to relationships, we find negative feedback in **complementary** relationships and positive feedback in **symmetrical** relationships.

Complementary relationships — fueled by negative feedback — include relationships between persons related by dominance-submission, exhibitionism-spectatorship, nurturance-dependence, and so forth, such as parents and children, bosses and employees, teachers and students, movie stars and fans. **Negative feedback** simply means that in such relationships interactions tend to **diminish** in intensity, with each interaction **subtracting** energy from the chain reaction. Just as someone riding a roller coaster or suspended from a bungee cord gradually comes to rest, so complementary relationships tend towards tranquillity.

There is a power differential in complementary relationships, so forgiveness usually means that the less powerful person will be the forgiven and the more powerful the forgiver. That is probably why such relationships tend towards stability. Here is where forgiveness with reconciliation is most likely to occur. But in complementary relationships the power differential also increases the likelihood that co-dependent counterfeits such as compliance, submission, appeasement, and fawning are also likely to occur.

Symmetrical relationships — fueled by positive feedback — always involve competition and tend to escalate. **Positive feedback** means that feedback from previous interactions tends to be additive and the relationship proceeds with increasing intensity. Symmetrical relationships include two boxers fighting, rival street gangs taunting each other, two children boasting that each is the strongest, or two alcoholics matching each other drink for drink at a bar. Symmetrical relationships with *others* easily escalate to high levels of tension. Arguments between people of all ages — toddlers or teens, middle-aged or retired — easily escalate to the level of shouting matches.

Forgiving allows you to break out of such symmetrical relationships by reframing the other person not as an opponent, enemy, or rival, but rather as one of God's children. This shifts you to a higher level of relationship; and just as a parent can play a game with a young child without seriously trying to win, forgiveness reframes symmetrical relationships to a higher context and eliminates the eyeball-to-eyeball intensity of competition.

Within oneself symmetrical loops — commonly known as "vicious circles" — are difficult to break. Such symmetrical struggles are like scratching an itch, which then itches more, which you then scratch more intensely, which subsequently itches even more until finally you end up with fingernail gouges in your still-itching skin.

Internal conflicts about whether to eat more food, drink more alcohol, or in other ways gratify ourselves are symmetrical struggles between our urges to gratify ourselves and prohibitions against such urges. Play vs. duty, gratification vs. inhibition, indulgence vs. abstinence — these are the evenly-matched boxers battling within us, and the more we obsess about how to win, the more intensely they fight.

The genius of Alcoholics Anonymous and self-help groups of similar genre is that they destabilize the *symmetrical loop* between *self* and *addiction*. Even the title — Alcoholics *Anonymous* —

diminishes the importance of the almighty self struggling against alcohol. This is consistent with a primary treatment ingredient — pointing the addict to a "higher power," which breaks the "vicious circle" of self vs. alcohol.

Reframing the problem by introducing outside help escapes the endless ping-pong game between self and alcohol by **disconnecting** from one's "weakness," "badness," or "lack of self- control" and reaching outside the confines of this symmetrical loop. Such disconnecting is a profound form of self-forgiveness.

Paul, the penetrating New Testament theologian, describes his inner struggles as a symmetrical loop between **self** and **sin**:

> *I do not understand what I do. For what I want to do I do not do, but what I hate I do.*
>
> *As it is, it is no longer I myself who do it, but it is sin living in me. I know that nothing good lives in me, that is, in my sinful nature. For I have the desire to do what is good, but I cannot carry it out. For what I do is not the good I want to do; no, the evil I do not want to do — this I keep on doing. Now if I do what I do not want to do, it is no longer I who do it, but it is sin living in me that does it.*
>
> *So I find this law at work: When I want to do good, evil is right there with me. For in my inner being I delight in God's law; but I see another law at work in the members of my body, waging war against the law of my mind and making me a prisoner of the law of sin at work within my members. What a wretched man I am! Who will rescue me from this body of death?* (Romans 7:15, 17-24)

Then he answers his own question and escapes his vicious circle with a reframe presaging Alcoholics Anonymous higher power:

> *Thanks be to God — through Jesus Christ our Lord! ... Therefore, there is now no condemnation for those who are in Christ Jesus, because through Christ Jesus the law of the Spirit of life set me free from the law of sin and death.* (Romans 7:25, 8:1-2)

Finally, after being rescued by his "higher power" he reaffirms his membership in the family of God:

> ... *because those who are led by the Spirit of God are sons of God. For you did not receive a spirit that makes you a slave again to fear, but you received the Spirit of sonship. And by him we cry, "Abba, Father." The Spirit himself testifies with our spirit that we are God's children. Now if we are children, then we are heirs — heirs of God and co-heirs with Christ, if indeed we share in his sufferings in order that we may also share in his glory.*
> (Romans 8:14-17)

Paul struggled not only to forgive himself for **inner mistakes** and **weaknesses**, he also had to forgive himself for **mistreating others**:

"For I am the least of the apostles and do not even deserve to be called an apostle, because I persecuted the church of God" (Corinthians 15:9). "... Christ Jesus came into the world to save sinners — of whom I am the worst" (1 Timothy 1:15).

Such memories could have been like heavy weights dragging him ever deeper into despair, but he exudes the energy of the forgiven when he declares: "Forgetting what is behind and straining toward what is ahead, I press on toward the goal to win the prize ... (Philippians 3:13, 14).

And in moving metaphors he suggests to his readers:

> ... *Clothe yourselves with compassion, kindness, humility, gentleness and patience. Bear with each other and forgive whatever grievances you may have against one another. Forgive as the Lord forgave you. And over all these virtues put on love, which binds them all together in perfect unity.* (Colossians 3:12-14)

Paul concludes that among the horde of transitory things in the cosmos, *love* (the fuel that propels forgiveness) will endure:

Love never fails. But where there are prophecies, they will cease; where there are tongues, they will be stilled; where there is knowledge, it will pass away ... And now these three remain: faith, hope and love. But the greatest of these is love. (1 Corinthians 13:8, 13)

Final Summary — Three Wishes

When doing psychotherapy with children I engage them in play, conversation, and games. Sometime in the first couple of sessions, I ask them to make three wishes. This gives me insight into how they view life, what's important to them, and helps me understand their problems more broadly. In a bit of a turnaround, I'd like to finish our journey by sharing with you **my three wishes**.

First wish: I hope **forgiving yourself and others will be easier** for you as a result of our journey together. Forgiveness is the oil of life, lubricating the gears of human interactions. Where forgiveness is plentiful things usually move smoothly. Without forgiveness, the daily mistakes and mistreatment we encounter grind and irritate us. With forgiveness, we find it easier to transcend trivia and the petty hurts of daily life. Forgiving frees us from the natural tendency to smolder with wrath or to seek revenge when wronged by others. Most importantly, forgiveness allows us to view our humanity in perspective and not view ourselves with contempt when we think of the many flaws in our own behavior.

If I've been successful in *reframing* forgiveness, you won't think of it as a teeth-grinding, fist-clenching act of sheer willpower; rather you'll understand it to be an *attitude* of living — an attitude that returns much of the benefit to you. The forgiver usually gets more out of it than the forgiven. So when you forgive, you'll find that it truly is "more blessed to give than to receive." You'll discover that by reframing, you'll be able to forgive more easily than ever before, and that when you do, it will be a "win-win" behavior with benefits for everyone. When it comes to forgiveness I hope you'll find it easy to follow Jesus' advice to His disciples: "Freely you have received, freely give" (Matthew 10:8).

Second wish: I hope you'll remember that **forgiving comes in many styles**, that it is an intricate *process* requiring time to ripen, and that different situations require different styles of this antidote. Stated succinctly, **forgiveness doesn't come in "one-size-fits-all."** Since human beings are destined to live by trial and error, we travel the journey of life best when equipped with ample supplies of forgiveness to deal with the inevitable mishaps along the way.

Just as the hiker's first aid kit supplies band-aids for blistered feet, cortisone cream for insect bites, and sunscreen to keep us from burning, forgiving enables us to cope with the multitude of minor irritations we encounter. But just as a well-supplied first aid kit contains tourniquets for severe bleeding and life-saving medication for those allergic to bee stings, forgiving is absolutely essential in the major crises of life, as when you inadvertently back up your automobile and kill the family pet (or, heaven forbid, your own child). It is almost impossible to endure such major misfortunes without generous doses of forgiveness.

Third wish: To live fully, with passion, one must **forgive completely**. So in addition to hoping that you'll forgive easily, in your own style, I hope you'll be able to **forgive decisively and irreversibly**. This is especially true in your own life. In the thirty years I've worked as a clinical psychologist, I've been disappointed in how often people obsessively re-view their personal failings and consequently how often they have to re-forgive themselves.

"Holding a grudge" against someone else is bad enough, because energy that's tied up with past issues is not available for present and future coping; but when you don't forgive *yourself* completely, the residual shame and guilt subtly sap your psychological energy just as surely as mononucleosis can sabotage your physical vigor. Hating others is tragic enough, but self-hatred is like HIV of the soul, destroying your ability to fight off despair, depression, hopelessness and a variety of other "pathogens" waiting to invade you.

I wish for you not merely that you survive, but that the healing power of forgiveness will enable you to live splendidly. May the flowers of forgiveness flourish in soil of your soul, blooming broadly and bringing (in the words of the prophet) "... a crown of beauty instead of ashes, the oil of gladness instead of mourning, and a garment of praise instead of a spirit of despair" (Isaiah 61:3).

And if perchance our paths have crossed, and I've mistreated you along the way, PLEASE PUT FLOWERS ON MY GRAVE. I may not smell their fragrance nor enjoy their colors, but *you* will. And like the gift of forgiveness they represent, flowers on my grave will make *your* life a bit easier, and the burdens *you* carry a bit lighter — until we meet again.

References

Arendt, H. (1958). *The human condition.* Chicago: The University of Chicago Press.

Arieti, S. (1974). *Interpretation of schizophrenia.* New York: Basic Books.

Ashby, W. R. (1961). *An introduction to cybernetics.* London: Chapman & Hall Ltd.

Bradshaw, J. (1988). *Healing the shame that binds you.* Deerfield Beach, FL: Health Communications.

Broucek, F. (1982). "Shame and its relationshp to early narcissistic development." *International Journal of Psycho-Analysis.* 65:369-378.

Davis, M. (1984). *It's hard to be humble.* New York: PolyGram Records, Inc.

Dobson, J. (1974). *Hide or seek.* Old Tappan, NJ: Revell.

Hampden-Turner, C. (1981). *Maps of the mind.* New York: Macmillan.

Jacobson, E. (1964). "The self and the object world: Vicissitudes of their infantile cathexis and their influences on ideational and affective development." *The Psychoanalytic Study of the Child,* 9:75-127. New York: Aronson.

Kaufman, G. (1985). *Shame the power of caring.* Rochester, VT: Schenkman Books, Inc.

Maslow, A.H. (1970). *Motivation and personality.* (2nd ed.) New York: Harper & Row.

157

May, R. (1977). "Freedom, determinism and the future." *Psychology, 1,* 6-9.

Morris, H. (1976). *On guilt and innocence.* Berkeley, CA: University of California Press.

Morrison, A.P. (1989). *Shame the underside of narcissism.* Hillsdale, NJ: The Analytic Press.

Nash, O. (1967). "If a boder meets a boder, need a boder cry? Yes," in *There's always another windmill.* Boston: Little, Brown and Company.

Nathanson, D. L. (Ed.). (1987). *The many faces of shame.* New York: Guilford Press.

The New International Version Study Bible. (1985). Grand Rapids, MI: The Zondervan Corporation.

Rapoport, J. L. (1989). *The boy who couldn't stop washing.* New York: Dutton.

Remarque, E. M. (1926). *All quiet on the western front.* Boston: Little, Brown and Company.

Rogers, C. R. (1959). "A theory of therapy, personality, and interpersonal relationships, as developed in the client-centered framework." In S. Koch (Ed.) *Psychology: A study of science (Vol. 3).* New York: McGraw-Hill.

Salzman, L. (1985). *Treatment of the obsessive personality.* Northvale, NJ: Aronson.

Shapiro, D. (1965). *Neurotic styles.* New York: Basic Books.

Shaver, K. G. (1985). *The attribution of blame: causality, responsibility, and blameworthiness*. New York: Springer-Verlag.

Skinner, B. F. (1948). *Walden two*. New York: Macmillan.

Smiley, J. (1991). *A thousand acres*. New York: Ballantine Books.

Tangney, J. P. (1993). *Shame-based anger: seeds of dysfunctional responses to interpersonal conflict*. Paper presented at the American Psychological Association meetings, Toronto, Canada.

Thielicke, H. (1959). *The waiting father*. New York: Harper & Row.

Thielicke, H. (1962). *Christ and the meaning of life*. New York: Harper & Row.

Toch, H. (1969). *Violent men: An inquiry into the psychology of violence*. Chicago: Aldine.

Twain, M. (1982). *The adventures of Tom Sawyer*. Berkeley, CA: University of California Press.

Watson, J. B. (1924). *Behaviorism*. New York: Norton.

Watson, M. A. Commentary for National Public Radio's *Morning Edition*, broadcast March 4, 1992.

Webster's Ninth New Collegiate Dictionary. (1983). Springfield, MA: Merriam-Webster Inc., Publishers.

Wheelis, A. (1973). *How people change*. New York: Harper & Row.

Winnicott, D. W. (1975). *Through paediatrics to psychoanalysis*. New York: Basic Books.

Wishnie, H. (1977). *The impulsive personality*. New York: Plenum.

Wurmser, L. (1981). *The mask of shame*. Baltimore, MD: Johns
   Hopkins University Press.